IESE Business Collection

The Palgrave Macmillan IESE Business Collection is designed to provide authoritative insights and comprehensive advice on specific management topics. The books are based on rigorous research produced by IESE Business School professors, covering new concepts within traditional management areas (Strategy, Leadership, Managerial Economics, etc.) as well as emerging areas of enquiry. The collection seeks to broaden the knowledge of the business field through the ongoing release of titles, with a humanistic focus in mind.

More information about this series at
http://www.palgrave.com/gp/series/14856

Beatriz Muñoz-Seca

How to Get Things Right

A Guide to Finding and Fixing Service Delivery Problems

Beatriz Muñoz-Seca
IESE Business School
Madrid, Madrid, Spain

Translated by Michael Martin Roberts

IESE Business Collection
ISBN 978-3-030-14087-8   ISBN 978-3-030-14088-5   (eBook)
https://doi.org/10.1007/978-3-030-14088-5

Library of Congress Control Number: 2019934473

This Palgrave Macmillan imprint is published by the registered company Springer Nature Switzerland AG
The registered company address is: Gewerbestrasse 11, 6330 Cham, Switzerland

To
All those who have worked side by side with me these past three years,
implementing SPDM ideas and getting it right. It was a true pleasure to be your
fellow traveler.

Contents

List of Figures

List of Tables

Introduction

Three years ago I finished my latest book entitled *How to Make Things Happen.* It had been a haphazard adventure entailing almost seven years' work on research, lecturing and assessing businesses. The above-mentioned book (with its corresponding practical application manual) outlines a conceptual scheme—service problem-driven management (SPDM). SPDM makes for understanding what Operations are in service companies and what essential "levers" a manager needs to pull in order to unblock the multiple situations slowing things down, or blocking them altogether, which arise while implementing a strategy.

The above-mentioned book ends with Cavafy's poem "Ithaka", which talks about the importance of undergoing a journey, after the fashion of Spanish poet Antonio Machado. I was pleasantly surprised over the holidays last year when one of my students from the 2018 Executive MBA[1] program at IESE wrote me the following in his final report on the "Operations Strategy" course:

> *This has been, definitely, my Cavafy-like journey to Ithaka over the last few months. It hasn't been too long, but it has been full of adventures, analyzing alternatives, experiences and, above all, learning. No Laestrygonians or Cyclops have appeared, but certain archetypes have done, as well as the odd Frankenstein. I haven't come across an angry Poseidon, either, since I have never had one among my brainpower. While short, the journey has taken me to unseen ports,*

---

[1] My readers know I cannot write without footnotes. This gives my editors headaches, but I need constantly to add comments. Here's the first one. It must be said that this student shares his thoughts with me in a very poetic way, which is not usual in the younger generation.

> *to sail across lakes of knowledge and stop at the green banks in Phoenicia to gaze at the mother-of-pearl and the coral, the amber and ebony, the sensual perfume or every kind. It has also given me the chance to walk the streets in Alexandria and set up indicators for following up the unit. I have co-created in Egyptian cities and enhanced my usefulness with the sages on the banks of the Nile. I have found in Ithaka the knowledge hub I was looking for and had to face up to the maddening residual uncertainty, armed only with a thousand $1000-improvements. Now, although Ithaka no longer has anything to offer me, it has indeed given me a beautiful journey. I am now a little older, but much wiser for what I have gathered on the way. Ithaka has not fooled me. Today I believe I am somewhat closer to understanding what Ithakas mean.*

Oddly, I feel the same way. For him it was four months on my course and for me three years since I finished my last book. Three years spent implementing ideas. Three years spent working side by side with several companies that chose to use them to get things right.[2] Three frankly fascinating years of very hard work. Above all, for seeing how the brains with which I worked adopted the ideas as their own[3] and used them to set up their own realities by smashing obstacles.

So here I am with the next book. To share with my readers how to get things right and what are the new ideas we have come up with between us. Ideas drawn up to unblock situations in which progress was lacking during implementation and in results. Therefore we have been adapting, inventing and offering practical solutions. Making challenges arise that were to be met in marathon sessions.[4] And now that we can look back and feel satisfied at a job well done, the time has come to share it.

This will not be a long book, and I mean to keep it down to under 200 pages. I am well aware that people don't read and that is why I want to make it brief.[5] I shall refer to the companies with which I have worked but not by their real names. I believe who they are is irrelevant, but what sectors they belong to does add value. They are a hotel company (Artemis[6]), one from the

---

[2] I have a thousand tales I shall try to tell. My previous book has a red cover for the simple reason that the "flame red" concept is one that hooks people. Then one day I heard someone say, in one of the companies that was implementing it, "Hey, have you got the red book? I need to look something up." It took two minutes for me to realize that they were talking about my book, because I am somewhat long in the tooth and thought they meant Chairman Mao's Little Red Book, which totally threw me.

[3] When someone tells you about an issue using your structure, and does so as if it were theirs and unbeknown to you, you know you have achieved your aim.

[4] I believe that many have ended up with physical problems, as we literally had no time for "concessions" (a term used in factories to denote bathroom breaks).

[5] As readers will appreciate: "short and sweet." Baltasar Gracián "Oráculo manual y arte de prudencia" 1647.

[6] Artemis: The Greek goddess of hunting.

gas distribution sector (Hephaestus[7]), a unit of a large bank (Achilles[8]) and a financial firm (Pegasus[9]). They are all Spanish. From abroad, an insurance company, an energy firm and a tourist operator.

This book has nine chapters whose title reenacts the problems with implementation that have arisen over these past three years of work.

1. The Operations puzzle
2. No Hire, No Fire: Address Sustainable Efficiency Before Headcount
3. Unlocking Capacity to Tackle Higher Value-Added Tasks
4. The Contribution Margin and Tribes
5. What Shall We Do With the Popups? On the Spot Innovation Can Create Unforeseen Problems
6. The Five-Star Constellation and Knowledge Pills
7. Problem-Solving Tracks and Service Modules
8. Altogether Now! We Need Everybody's Effort Implementing the "9 Questions" Tool
9. Concluding Thoughts

A brief summary of the content.

We shall begin with the need to understand the puzzle to be built. Implementing a strategy forces you to understand all the operative components in play. Its pieces, its joints, its design and its framing.

We shall begin with a great opportunity available to us nowadays: technology opens the way for human beings to do greater value-added jobs, and the NO HIRE, NO FIRE principle should be the "battle cry" in this so-called fourth industrial and services revolution.[10] The main thrust will become *unlocking capacity* in order to take on greater value-added jobs and letting machines work 24/7 on their jobs. Unlocking capacity does away with ever-present comments like "I can't cope with it" or "I haven't the time". It is the sine qua non for beginning implementation.

In the coming pages we shall delve into a world of adventure: understanding clients' anthropological profile based on their tribes. This approach makes for designing a services portfolio while thinking about each tribe's contribution margin, and provides a new way of looking at old problems.

---

[7] Hephaestus: The Greek god of fire and forges
[8] Achilles: Hero of the Trojan War, invulnerable in all of his body except his heel.
[9] Pegasus: Winged horse and the first horse that came to be alongside the Greek gods.
[10] Please take note. Apart from industry and its Industry 4.0 concept, the impact on services is just as revolutionary.

When we talk about popups, it won't be to delve into the world of computing. In this book popups are the spontaneous innovations that arise in companies. This chapter reveals their existence and analyzes ways to catch them before they appear. The help and involvement of the recipient of innovation/change, the so-called innosufferer, is an essential requirement for achieving sustainable implementation. Their role becomes the mainstay when implementing.

Involving the innosufferer means attacking the so-called Five-Star Constellation. This lovely term entails blending knowledge stock, analyzing each agent's capacities and forecasting knowledge needs and specific training plans, in order to solve today's and tomorrow's problems. The knowledge pills concept will arise, a way to provide training aimed at solving concrete problems.

The structure required for sustainable implementation in this century, which is ever full of movement and upheavals, must be flexible and adaptable. These are the so-called problem-solving tracks. This track or freeway concept must be combined with setting up service modules that make for breaking down services into independent units, which may be internally or externally managed in the extended enterprise.

We finish with the battle cry "Altogether now!" to explain the need to accept everybody in executing implementation. Getting every piece of the puzzle to know what is in it for them, to explain what causes everything until you're tired of it and to be patient and persistent become essential for getting it right.

Some concluding thoughts in order to put the finishing touches. They are a summary of what I deem most important for getting it right. A round-up to be pondered, and in order to spot what may begin to be implemented right away.

At the end of each chapter there is a reference to SPDM concepts. By the same token, I have drawn on the SPDM manual the formulas that go with the concepts described in each chapter. I confine myself to describing and referring to them to allow the reader to analyze them, if she/he so chooses.

Before I begin each chapter, the relevant acknowledgments. To my daughters and sons-in-law, for pulling through with me these past three years. To those with whom I have worked, for putting up with marathon sessions and demands. To all who have put up with me. Being a long-in-the-tooth professor has its advantages and disadvantages.

Reasons for Writing this Book

Let us spell out what this book is about from the very start. It is short-sighted to think you can get results leading to operational efficiency merely by looking at cost-cutting and replacing people with technology.[1] Completely and totally short-sighted.

We are facing a great opportunity: ***To give our people higher value-added jobs that boost the company's contribution margin, and provide them with new knowledge that will make them more employable.*** No hire, no fire until you have extracted total and absolute operating efficiency, until you have relieved your people of jobs that a machine can do much more efficiently and consistently, until you have freed brainpower from jobs that add little value and prevent them producing much more. That is the challenge. Win-win. Company and employee both. A wonderful situation that allows us to focus on productive action by doing away with time-wasting, something totally unsatisfying and frustrating for all concerned.

To solve this problem we begin with a capacity analysis where each agent's occupancy rate may be seen. And the one that consumes least on one of the tasks is then the benchmark. We don't look for the inefficient ones, but the efficient ones instead, so they can show the rest. Because it is all about solving today's and tomorrow's problems productively. And for that we must apply the necessary knowledge stock. There is nowhere to focus efficiency without using knowledge. There is no way to broach readjusting jobs and introducing technology, without broaching how to produce solutions more deftly. To wit,

---

[1] Yes, costs will be cut. Yes, the year-end bottom line will be salvaged. But, at what price? Maybe tomorrow's efficiency, and certainly today's.

broaching efficiency is not sustainable unless it is linked to using knowledge for problem-solving.

These ideas suffuse the whole book. I shall summarize them in the following box to turn them into a narrative, because it is a simple and powerful message.

> A worker is "brainpower" that must perform value-added tasks rather than jobs that a machine can do more efficiently. The union of human and machine is the twenty-first century's thrilling challenge. Companies must go hand-in-hand with their people during this transition, and thus they must understand the scope of operating strategy. There is no room for inefficient structures, overlapping or wastage. Nimble and adaptable operations are required, whose mainstay is using knowledge to solve service problems, today and tomorrow. Employability is what everybody gets out of it, and for that each agent's capacity must be unlocked so that they can use it to make their company progress, as well as themselves.

That is the overriding message of "getting" it right.

The companies introduced in this book are committed[2] to this narrative, and they all understand that efficiency without such engagement will get them nowhere. They have found that to get results, you have to send the message that transformation is focused on value added and getting rid of waste. It is an engaging and convincing narrative. Brainpower gets irritated when doing jobs that contribute nothing while they wish to face new challenges. And that is the way to "sell" restructuring to enhance operational efficiency.

The sequence is simple. First analyze capacities and occupancy rate. Then spot jobs to be automated or substituted by technology. Next, do your planning and a rolling forecast of today and tomorrow's knowledge stock to solve today and tomorrow's problems.

Then we can now delve into other issues entailed in the SPDM model, such as service design and clients' hidden needs.

For those that have not read my previous book, I shall now present a very brief summary of my conceptual model. You may skip this part if you wish, but I have introduced it to make reading the chapters easier. I shall mention

---

[2] Let us be frank, more or less intensely. They range from complete "zealots" to those that have to be convinced.

SPDM elements[3] constantly, and although I summarize the SPDM concepts used at the end of each chapter, the summary outlined below may be of use.

Madrid, Spain   Beatriz Muñoz-Seca

---

[3] I am sorry, but SPDM has its own special vocabulary and the previous book had a small dictionary of terms. I appreciate that this particular idiom does not make for easy understanding, but I have had to devise it to ensure succinct messages get through.

Methodology and Summary of Service Problem-Driven Management (SPDM)

A very summarized summary of Service Problem-Driven Management (SPDM) with hints of new developments revealed in this book.

Operations includes everything leading from an idea to a satisfied client. Strategy defines Operations, and thus the latter must follow unswervingly the indications defined by the strategic principles.

But the strategy must be "translated" into priorities that every member of the organization can understand; what for? Well, to prioritize actions. Absent such translating and prioritizing, company agents will do things their own way, or by common sense,[1] and the outcome will be truly disastrous for sustainable efficiency.

Making the strategy happen requires understanding the Operations components in order to understand the link between them. Without an Operations model in mind, implementing strategy is not possible.

The SPDM model (Muñoz-Seca 2017) outlines a conceptual framework for acting. The SPDM structure sets out three levels of action and settings (Fig. 1) that range from very concrete operational actions to very abstract thought, spotting the company's knowledge stock and translating the operational strategy. Half-way between both levels lies the service settings design. As a transversal mainstay required in order to be able to achieve implementation, we propose problem equals knowledge. *Thus understood, knowledge becomes the cornerstone of sustainable efficiency.* Solving service problems today

---

[1] Common sense does not exist. It is the stock of experience and learning that makes each person take decisions according to their own personal criteria. Determining actions by using it is inefficient. Decision-making criteria must be defined.

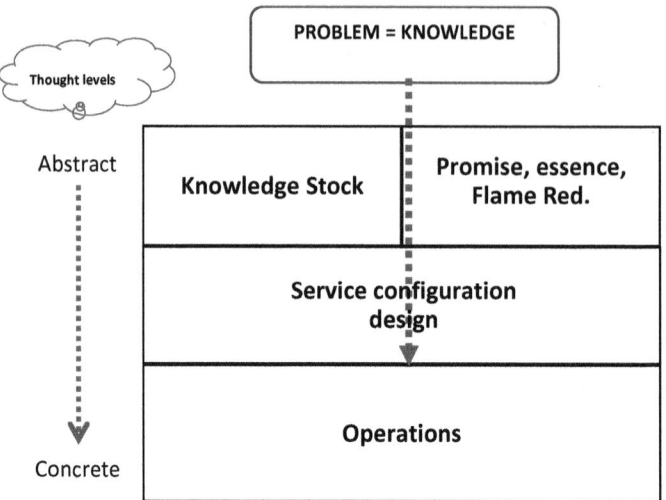

Fig. 1 SPDM (Muñoz-Seca 2017)

and tomorrow makes ideas happen. And for that each agent must know how to do so.

A lightning tour of SPDM would be as follows:

The company strategy must be translated into the Promise. A company promises clients a service and every member of the organization must be aware of that Promise.

Making the Promise happen on a day-to-day basis requires breaking it down into five dimensions, which in turn must be translated into each company's specific idiom or vocabulary. Cost, time, range, innovation and consistency are these five dimensions. And the specific translation can range from the contribution margin (cost), service time, between the client asking and receiving (time), services portfolio (range), number of new services obtained in each quarter (innovation), to reliability in specifying the promised service (consistency).

Once the Promise has been broken down, the CEO/MD must prioritize those dimensions. The aim is to provide criteria for agents to choose those problems that have the most impact on the company's Promise.[2] And everybody pulls together to implement successfully and in harmony. If the CEO does not do this job, the rest of the organization will proceed by common

---

[2] Making it unnecessary to use personal criteria or, for that matter, common sense.

sense, with the disastrous outcome that an agent might think they are choosing the most relevant problem, when this is really not so.

The Promise, with its five dimensions and their translation, is the first essential step toward obtaining effective implementation.

Once the strategy has been translated, management must determine the company's essence and flame red. The essence is defined by a word or very short phrase, what sets each company apart. That is its DNA, what must permeate every pore in client interactions and the relationship between agents. Trust, transparency and being close to details are some of companies' essences.

Essence is based on the flame red. The flame red is that part of the operational structure that makes the essence happen. For example, an essence of "trust" may have its flame red in the suppliers' management area, "transparency" in the information systems area, "being close to details" in the office staff.

Having gone through this first filter, we proceed to the "operational" layer to look for sustainable efficiency. As a first step, every agent's occupancy rate in the organization must be found. Capacity analysis is the gateway to analyzing operational variables and allows endless wastage to be unraveled.[3] Determining agents' occupancy[4] shows the lowest consumption needed to do jobs. The latter are then the benchmark for all the other agents, as long as they uphold the Promise's priority criteria.

The link between knowledge and efficiency becomes visible when the "best consumption" is determined. Whoever does something best does so because they apply knowledge specific to solving problems. And that knowledge becomes the cornerstone to be shared with others. This gives *knowledge an essential role in SPDM as the mainstay for making things happen*. Embedded in this approach is demanding that everything that can be industrialized is industrialized. Agents are "brainpower" that needs to be freed from unnecessary frustrations that arise from inefficiencies present in their everyday work, and/or low value-added jobs they must do.

Occasionally, operational analysis will come across blockages that are impossible to fix solely by using efficiency. The basic principles of service design need to be understood, and the situation must be turned upside down to look at it from a totally different angle. SPDM builds service design using the Service Activities Sequence (SAS). The SAS envisages the array of actions required to unblock the above-mentioned problem and deliver the desired service. It starts by conceptualizing and prototyping the service. Next, the

---

[3] It is like pulling on a thread to unravel a ball of yarn.
[4] For that we use the Greek letter rho: ρ.

infrastructure is set up to help agents solve problems according to their knowledge needs. Then the operational structure is set up, along with its key performance indicators (KPIs). Then, the service provision components are generated and the variables intrinsic in constant improvement are analyzed. Finally, clients' hidden demands are found with the aim of creating new services that provide answers to the latter. This final step is the so-called service golden gate. Agents providing the service draw out clients' latent demands and they spawn a very important ideas base for designing new services. These new ideas must be incorporated[5] when conceptualizing the service, thus spawning proposals that add value.

The wholesale implementation of SPDM requires a management style totally opposed to "Do what I say". It stems from the concept that "to manage is to serve", but requires brainpower to be led by a firm hand along with transparency and consistency. There is no room for petty games.[6] Getting it right requires focus and clear priorities.

I should like to finish by introducing new cast members. SPDM is alive and well, and these past three years we have shaped issues sketched out in the previous book, and issues that have arisen out of the need to solve problems with implementation. Service modules were newborns in my previous book and have now been through childhood. The same goes for tracks, new settings to boost agility and adapt to service demand. The innosufferer, also previously introduced, has acquired a leading role in approaches to implementation analyzed these past three years. The Five-Star Constellation and "knowledge pills" have also come about. I have found many "popups" in response to brainpower's frustration or individualism. The features so essential to brainpower have allowed me to spot a new syndrome, the "Himalaya" syndrome, which defines specific ad hoc behavior. All this will be explained and analyzed in the book's chapters.

Summarizing 7+3 years' hard work in three pages is no mean feat. I hope to have provided the reader with a quick outline, garnished with hints of the new concepts presented in this book. Both will allow the conceptual base for SPDM to be understood.

---

[5] This must be done using a Service Innovation Cycle, CIS, which links latent demands to concept design.
[6] Endless power games cannot and must not be tolerated. They add no value, just unproductive time consumption and a great deal of frustration.

A Brief Synopsis of the Working Methodology Used with the Companies Involved

The working method used with the companies is based on the educational principles of active learning. Given that adults learn by solving problems, participants are provided with a conceptual and methodological approach that allows them to spot, unravel and solve problems.

The mainstay of action is making implementation happen. Work is not confined to analyzing and diagnosing. Work is concentrated mainly on solving and implementing. Therefore, we seek results constantly that demonstrate progress as we go. Quick-wins that are win-win. And all by following the sacred keep it simple and stupid (KISS) principle. The simpler, the better.

Implementation is made to happen by the person who shows how to adapt solutions. To do that, we work on three methodological fronts:

- Efficiency. Solving operational problems that cause inefficiencies and productivity shortfalls. Such problems irritate brainpower.
- Personal learning and company learning. Brainpower needs to learn and feel that it enhances personal growth every time it solves service efficiency problems. An organization needs to understand that it is learning and looking at problems under a different light, which provides it with operational solutions.
- Unit. People must identify with and feel part of the project's priorities. For that we must implement "do-do" by using a proactive problem-solving style that concerns everybody and makes learning important.

Each company that goes down this road with me sets up a working group (base group) that will be on the receiving end of SPDM methodology. This group works side by side with the author and owns the transformation. The group participants, in turn, set up other groups to snowball the learning effect.

Each SPDM project, in each company, has someone in charge of ensuring that milestones are reached on time and of spotting blockages that need smashing and to keep analyzing the development of the agreed work program together with the author.

The rules of the game are as follows:

- The one in charge of the project takes part in every group and keeps track of the work done and milestones reached.

- The groups take charge of solving the problems given to them and of implementing the solutions they propose.
- They work with achievable milestones, indicators, deliverables and expected results.
- They receive methodological transmission, as well as support in spotting knowledge gaps and transmitting SPDM concepts.
- Each group's proposals are handed to the base group, which must analyze them for approval.
- Solutions are followed up pro-actively, while proceeding by continuous prototyping and a lean start-up approach. That will allow a learning curve to be drawn, implementations to be tested and realities to be adapted.

The work group proceeds with clear aims that stem from dysfunctions found in implementing the Promise and/or concrete efficiency targets. The company CEO or MD plays a very important role. This individual specifies the Promise's priorities and provides the strategic view of the need for the work that the group will tackle. The CEO may be closely linked to the development of the work group by taking an active part in it, or may stay more on the sidelines, but be briefed constantly on progress achieved.

SPDM provides a methodological structure that guides each participant along his/her particular problem-solving path. Each problem is provided with a conceptual basis, a diagnosis and assessment of alternatives. Bearing in mind that each brainpower has a different approach to understanding problems, and based on the conceptual outline of the Educational Dimensions Portfolio,[7] work is almost made to measure for participants.

Having a common, clear and concise focus is indispensable. Unless done at the beginning of the project, an intensive session is held to unravel the origins of service problems.

The work done in each company is its group work. The author confines herself to steering the learning process, assessing solutions, providing the way to focus work and adding a conceptual outline so that each participant can find their own solution, and so that the group can seek synergies in joint solutions. To do the work, innovations are often needed to solve previously unidentified situations. This exploratory work is done jointly where the author contributes her experience and mental model to support methodological solutions that help to solve situations.

---

[7] EDP (Muñoz-Seca 2008; Muñoz-Seca and Silva Santiago 2003) offers four alternatives for beginning the learning process. These are providing experiences, analyzing alternatives, providing knowledge and supporting the process.

It is therefore a "do-do" approach, teach and learn. Each person owns their solution and thereby a very high level of engagement in the work and its aims is obtained.

When the project is finished, the group has made the SPDM methodology its own, has modified and adapted it to their overall context and made it part of their operational culture. The problems initially spotted have been solved and the group and its knock-on effects are prepared to face new challenges.

Implementing solutions is a vital piece in the puzzle for empirically determining the conceptual model's worth, and how solutions contribute different proposals for dealing with problems. Thinking "outside the box" is one of SPDM's great contributions.

List of Key Actors

Adriano: Head of Fixed Income at Achilles, leader of the I-CAN project and G-12 member.

Ana: G12 member and in charge of spotting "suffering" situations in implementation processes at Achilles. Dubbed the "innosufferer".

Achilles: Banking company, leading player in this book.

Artemis: Hotel company, leading player in this book.

Cristina: HR manager at Hephaestus and head of the Five-Star Constellation project at Hephaestus.

G12:   Group of 12 members of Achilles in charge of implementing the Transformation project.

Hephaestus: Gas company, leading player in this book.

Juan: Head of Emergencies at Hephaestus.

María: G12 member and head of the Voicing Client Specifications (VCS) project.

Pegasus: Financial firm, leading player in this book

70 tutees: Individuals in Achilles who implement the Transformation Plan as a knock-on effect from G12.

1

The Operations Puzzle

Abstract Operations lead from an idea to a satisfied customer. They are company strategy translated into reality. This chapter shows how the four leading players in this book have translated their strategies into operational priorities. The first step of this journey is Promise, essence and flame red.

Let us begin our journey. The first thing is to look for our destination and the course[1] we will take. Our destination is the company's permanent sustainability. The compass that keeps us on course is what I call the Operations puzzle. Without that, we shall make way haphazardly and without using what I reckon is the lean war cry: "avanti, avanti".[2]

Starting Point

One of the owners of Artemis, a medium-sized Family hotel company, told me: "SPDM has given me a blueprint that lets me see what I am not doing and the impact that has on what I am doing. It is a great help to be able to ask hotel managers accurately and understand where the problem arises. I have found that we have a problem in maintaining my family's "essence". We have six hotels with one owner, but not a group of six hotels."

---

[1] Using the dictionary definition: "Direction taken or plotted on the horizontal plane, and mainly any point on the compass card."

[2] It sounds much nicer in Italian. But ever onward, never turning back.

© The Author(s) 2019
B. Muñoz-Seca, *How to Get Things Right*, IESE Business Collection,
https://doi.org/10.1007/978-3-030-14088-5_1

Getting six hotels to have the same essence, when they had different locations and hotel rankings, made working with basic SPDM concepts obligatory: essence, service dream, Promise and flame red.

Each of Artemis's hotel managers had left their mark with the help of a Family member. The Family had been involved in each hotel's day-to-day running and that enabled transmitting part of the essence. Priorities were spotted and decisions taken as this daily relationship went along. The Family wanted to prepare a legacy for the next generation and was thus immersed in "professionalizing" the service's operational management. The grandparents' original essence seemed to be slipping away. Translating it here and now showed up disparities that could lead to a loss in Artemis's differential. Members that had been with Artemis for more than ten years felt the essence emotionally, but it was not rationally spelled out. It had been transmitted by word of mouth and that is very subjective.

After undertaking a study with the proprietors, the Family's essence was spotted as, "At everybody else's service." The Family wanted a service based on Family ties and a personal invitation to each client, as if they were guests at the Family home itself.

The work done to rationalize and spot the service essence was translated as "The Artemis Family invites you." The Family wanted to transmit their essence whether it was to a three-, four- or five-star hotel. For that, they had to break down the essence into five commandments:

1. The people serving you are happy and guests feel positive energy when interacting.
2. The manager and managing team are the hosts.
3. The surroundings breathe harmony, relaxation and comfort.
4. In balance with nature.
5. Developing "the art of caring for and serving others" by conveying personally our pleasure to serve and making the experience in an Artemis establishment unique, gratifying and inspirational.

Spotting the essence also made the Family define their service dream. The latter materialized as, "When clients go home, they dream of coming back to our hotels."

And what was the mainstay in supporting this essence? After a good many discussions,[3] it was understood that the mainstay (the company's flame red)

---

[3] Stemming from the central offices' role and how that was redefined in giving service to those who were really the mainstay: each hotel's managers.

Table 1.1 Artemis's Promise and evaluated dimensions

Range: Service provision	4
Personalized treatment + immediate response to client requests	
Friendliness	
Sensations experienced	
F&B: above-average raw material specified	
Consistency: Reliability	2
In-service provision	
Specifying individual client treatment (manners)	
Innovation: New ideas for daily services. Creativity	2
Cost: Overall service margin	1
Time: Agility in making decisions	1
Total score	10

was the hotel managers. They constituted the essence's watchdogs, an extension of the Family that had to commune with that essence to transfer it to everybody at the moments of truth (MT) when interacting with clients. But by giving each manager a free hand? Obviously not. More detail was needed.

That came hand in hand with defining the Promise. The Family and the CEO defined the Promise as "Faithfully providing clients with what they chose our hotel for." As there were six hotels, each with its special features, translating the Promise was indispensable. Each tourist category hotel would specify its own services portfolio, but Promise and essence would be left alone.

The organization had to be given clear guidelines, which would snowball to enable action and prioritization[4] in keeping with wishes as expressed. To that end the Promise was broken down into its dimensions, which were evaluated[5] in order of priority.[6] They had to be translated into reality to deliver a clear mandate for action (Table 1.1).

We see that the most important dimension is range of service provision (4/10). This translates into personalized treatment, friendly treatment to clients, a customer journey with sensations and food and beverage (F&B) with above-average raw material as a starting point.

The two following dimensions with the highest score are service reliability and new ideas for service provision (both 2/10). Spotting new opportunities for service provision (clients' so-called latent demands) must be done while providing the service itself.

---

[4] Each team in each hotel translated the essence in its own way. That prompted behavior that we might call "surprising".

[5] The Family was given ten points, and each member evaluated each dimension. Next, the average was found and consensus was reached with everybody over that score.

[6] The Family played the leading role in this job. The CEO wanted them to fully engage with the prioritizing process.

Although lean decision-making was given a low score by the Family, the group spotted it as a very important problem due to its impact on their workaday lives. Sluggishness hindered many service provision activities, and the group figured that that should be streamlined. That led to measures to tackle that inefficiency.

Just by looking at the highest-scoring dimension (service provision), it may be clearly seen that two essential jobs needed to be done: first, specifying the "whole customer journey" from which critical interaction points could be discerned in order to standardize, harmonize and industrialize; second, unlocking directors' capacity[7] to focus them on minding essence and service provision. Unlocking capacity that way also allowed all other dimensions to be fulfilled better. Transforming directors into service watchdogs meant that they spent time on taking action over reliability and improvement as new ideas for daily services.[8]

In work sessions held with the hotel managers, actions were pored over that could be taken to boost implementing these priorities and to smash blocking factors that prevented them from happening.[9] As a priority, Artemis worked hard to tackle unlocking managers' capacity, as well as the customer journey.

Noteworthy efforts were made to materialize essence and transmit it to every hotel employee. To that end, a questionnaire was designed and filled in personally by everybody that had worked at Artemis for more than ten years. The questionnaire analyzed how the Family addressed each of those surveyed, how they interrelated with clients, what service details the Family stressed most, the details of physical appearance they found most important,[10] the personal interface behavior the Family had with clients and employees, or how they behaved in conflictive situations. The questionnaire wanted to spot

---

[7] Some of them had already internalized that essence in their almost daily dealings with the Family. The challenge was in materializing all this informal knowledge in such a way that it could be transmitted to new hires. Keeping it inside a few heads that refused to materialize it was a big risk.

[8] Readers should not confuse a hotel chain with a company owning a small number of hotels. Nonetheless, in both cases the service watchdog must be the manager. I have stayed in a great many hotels in my professional life. In almost none have I had personalized treatment when revisiting. At one stage in my life I used to carry a little card with my room requirements printed on it, and would hand it in at reception, saying: "You'd better come up with this otherwise you'll have me here demanding it until I get it." And as some people know, perseverance is one of my traits. Result: I got check-in staff to remember me when I revisited because of that particular trait. Good service? No, awful and frankly very boring to waste time over.

[9] In later chapters in this book, we shall run through the actions that were designed.

[10] Tattoos, for example. It is very hard to find young people without some tattoo or other. This did not go down well because it did not transmit the required tone. Therefore, ways were found to cover them up by not allowing short sleeves, so as to hide them. Obviously, there was no room for body piercing in this backdrop. One team member told me that he thought that was old-fashioned so I told him one of my

Table 1.2 Scores in Artemis's service

I. Honesty and transparency
Integrity in each and every situation we shall develop
II. Diligence
Facing every adversity we come across professionally and reliably
III. Taking responsibility
We shall do our jobs relentlessly and unfailingly: we shall always find solutions
IV. Effort
Any challenge can be met with the personal ability and means the company has available
V. Loyalty
Whatever our function may be, we owe the company: Integrity, allegiance, reliability and respect
VI. Daring
Any situation can be faced using everybody's individual attitude and aptitudes

critical elements materialized from the essence to then be reflected in the welcome pack that was handed[11] out annually.

The questionnaires' results were tabulated and shared in a session with all the hotel managers, who commented and voiced their opinions. It was decided that the Family essence must be conveyed to all the Operations manuals that were being revamped and had to become an integral part of training courses at Artemis. By the same token, developing apps was mooted to enable implementation, and the daily use of manuals using portable devices. Every worker had to have access to the essence's definition as well as to how the Promise was clarified and evaluated. One element was missing in order to translate the essence: behavior rules for the operational culture. The latter had to be based on the above-mentioned five commandments and the Family's service values. The same group was asked again what values had been transmitted to them in their work during Artemis's 50-year life. They were found to be honesty and transparency; diligence; taking responsibility; effort; loyalty and daring. Table 1.2 articulates them with a description of how they are understood at Artemis.

Macro performance rules for Artemis's operations culture were derived from these values (Table 1.3). These operations rules were submitted to the managers and department heads at head office. They were commented on, discussed and accepted as behavioral guidelines. Accepted by all, they were industrialized and transmitted in the welcome pack that all the company's workers received when they began work for the season.

---

favorite personal anecdotes. When I began to work in the USA an age ago, my company CEO called me into his office and said: "You European ladies insist in going around in summer without stockings on. Here in Texas, everybody wears stockings to work, it is impolite not to do so." Point taken, those were company rules and I had to follow them. Exactly the same applies in those hotels.

[11] Remember that in the catering sector there is a lot of turnover and the so-called fixed discontinuous hiring. That makes it very important to be able to transmit essence industrially for new hires to "breathe" the DNA from day one.

Table 1.3 Operations macro rules for Artemis's service

Values		Operations macro rules
I. Honesty and transparency	1	There are no culprits: there are situations
	2	Every situation must be fact based
	3	Be true to one's word and take on commitments
	4	Commit and express oneself consistently and authentically
II. Diligence	5	Don't leave for tomorrow what you can do today
	6	Perseverance and conscientiousness at work
	7	Those that want to do something find a way: those that do not find an excuse
III. Taking responsibility	8	More freedom, more responsibility
	9	Take on difficulties as they arise
IV. Effort	10	The word impossible is meaningless
	11	Sacrifice may achieve little, but nothing is achieved without it
V. Loyalty	12	At Artemis ideas are transmitted clearly and respectfully
VI. Daring	13	Face difficulties bravely and boldly
	14	Do not look aside

Piecing Together the Puzzle

Spotting Promise, essence, flame red and the service dream is all indispensable for making things happen. But not enough. Making things happen requires having a complete picture of the whole mosaic of actions taken, including each one's cross-impact. Managers' great bugbear with Operations is that improving one component then affects others in unsuspected ways, normally for the worse. It is like a domino. If the mosaic is not understood, the implications cannot be foreseen. And the effect is terrifying because action comes after the fact, not preventively. In Operations, you must act five minutes ahead, be proactive and on top of those Operations. Never forget that Operations mean taking thousands of decisions, and if managers will not decide, someone else will instead.[12]

Making things happen means understanding the whole Operations puzzle. What is the Operations puzzle? Let us take a good look at Pegasus to understand what we are talking about.

Pegasus, our financial firm, had part of its operations settings in third parties on which it depended to get results and make things happen. This is the so-called extended enterprise[13] ecosystem. It is very common practice in services. The service does not only depend on the company itself, but on the

---

[12] And with the best will in the world that decision may be wrong. At times, they are taken from a micro viewpoint when they have macro implications.

[13] Extended Enterprise (Moss Kanter 1999). A totally integrated concept in SPDM. It takes into account the ecosystem of companies making up the service.

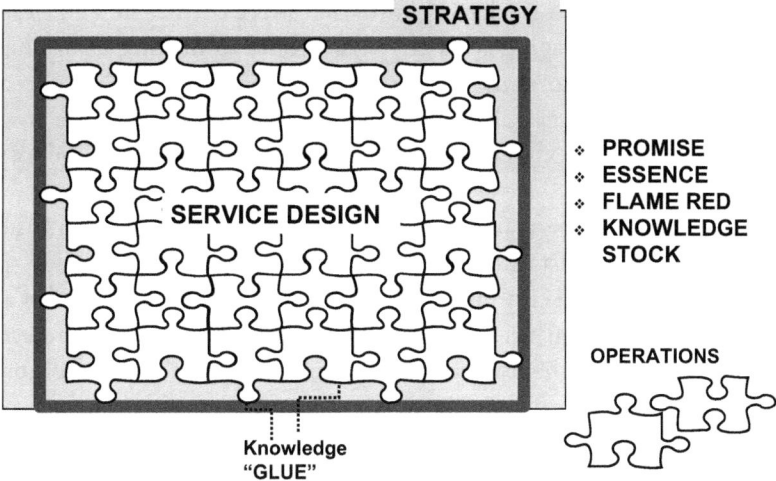

Fig. 1.1 The Operations puzzle

aggregate of services from a cluster of companies that make up the extended enterprise ecosystem.[14]

At Pegasus, that link had been set up using an exhaustive contract designed by the legal department, based on every requirement that each department had imagined could exist. The contract had given rise to multiple Service Level Agreements (SLAs)[15] and a unit directly responsible for following them up had to be established. Neither the contract nor the SLAs got the expected results.

Upon analyzing the knowledge contributed by each partner[16] to achieve the contract's aims, it was found that not only was knowledge often duplicated in Pegasus and its partners, but that Pegasus at times ended up doing the partner's job. All out of despair to achieve response times. Applying more SLAs would not fix the situation. The operational settings needed to be delved into thoroughly to spot what stopped at Pegasus and what was handed to the extended enterprise. No more duplication or inefficiency.

The Operations puzzle (Fig. 1.1) is a picture drawn to understand the inherent complexity in devising an operational strategy. Building an

---

[14] One or multiple companies may provide the service. When part of the service is handed to third parties, we call it an extended enterprise and talk of the ecosystem that comprises that swarm of companies. The AVE (Spanish high-speed train) is a good example of this, because whereas Ferroser provides the on-board service and handles passengers, clients think it is an AVE service. And so it is, albeit provided by a third party.

[15] SLA, Service Level Agreement. Service indicators agreed between companies by contract.

[16] Member of the extended enterprise ecosystem. We use that term to transfer the link when delivering the service.

Operations strategy means delving into each piece's structure and designing each one's fit, by envisaging what they contribute to making things happen. Operations are there to make the strategy's wishes happen. And the operational settings needed to fulfill those wishes may be found in the company itself, as well as in the extended one. The assembly will make up the total and whole service.

As Fig. 1.1 shows, managing Operations means managing parts of the puzzle that are blurred constantly and must be reset. It is an amoeba-like[17] puzzle that must be readjusted constantly. Understanding whether the foot of a piece or the assembly design has been modified is essential to enable resetting it quickly and achieving the desired effect. A poor diagnosis of the assembly may fix one piece, in the short term, but ruin ten.

The puzzle stems from the framework imposed by strategy (Fig. 1.1). Said framework defines what the company wants to be best at and what its differential is. The strategy leads, Operations follow and translate to make things happen. To do this, the framework must be translated into understandable and bearable language for the whole organization: the Promise with its priorities, essence and flame red. Along with that, knowledge is now essential in twenty-first-century Operations. The latter cannot be designed without bearing in mind what the company knows and what it does not know and must know to make the strategy happen. Curiously, Pegasus had a problem with excess knowledge stock. This meant that people tended to enter into micro details and perform tasks that were really not up to them and had been contracted out to the extended enterprise. This turned out to be totally inefficient.

Once the aforesaid components are spotted, the natural trend is to move on directly to the operations structure, to each piece of the puzzle. Problems erupt at this level and the urgent need to fix them takes over. And it is right to intervene piece by piece, but on the understanding that the eruption is usually down to poor design of the joint between the pieces, that is, the service design. The problems stem from the pieces, but the fit between them spawns many misunderstandings and mismatches. Service design must take into account not only the service provided by the company itself but also that provided by the extended one. The ecosystem is one, and all of the pieces are parts of the puzzle.

Directly translating the operations strategy without first designing the service has very harmful consequences. Defining operations elements, like

---

[17] Don't ask me why, but I have been a great fan of amoebas since an early age. Maybe because the amoeba's main feature is that it has no cell wall, so its shape varies, and that adaptability, together with osmosis, has fascinated me.

capacities or the information system, without first analyzing what is the Promise's priority dimension, what knowledge stock is needed to solve problems or what is the best way to design the service, leads to "Frankenstein"[18] solutions. And the tragedy is not only that it is not aesthetically pleasing, but that either resources are being wasted or the service is failing. The company and the extended enterprise must be consolidated in the service design, and then Frankenstein solutions will disappear by smashing inefficiencies.

When I began to work with Pegasus, response time was the most important factor when the Promise was not kept. Time compression was tackled by eliminating inefficiency and duplication, and doing some "spring cleaning".[19] Six work groups were set up that met in a room specially designed for the project, where, drawn on the wall, the whole process's components from start to finish could be seen, without bearing in mind what department they belonged to. The more-than-60 people who threw themselves into time compression had a clear focus: time. There were no questionnaires and the message was concise, and created a powerful driving force. They plunged into the parts of the puzzle, because that is where the eruptions had to be controlled.

When results began to emerge and part of the tension eased, it transpired clearly that the cause of the problems was the settings of Pegasus + extended enterprise's service design. This could not have been found until the fog, which had been produced by all the operational inefficiencies that affected response time, lifted. It was necessary to go down to the level of the pieces in the puzzle to understand their structure and see their inefficiencies.

After cleaning up the pieces, it was obvious that their fit needed to be overhauled. And this is the service design that must be guided by prioritizing the strategy materialized in the Promise, and by clearly spelling out the company's essence or DNA.

Moreover, Pegasus spotted that its differential did not come from having each piece's specific knowledge; it left the latter to the extended enterprise. Pegasus had to reinvent itself as a knowledge hub[20] highly specialized in tiresome problems. By the same token, it needed the glue, or knowledge required to join all the pieces in the puzzle to allow it to be seen as a whole.

---

[18] I introduced this concept years ago when I saw the situations I came across. True operational monsters. I see that the term has taken off in the press lately, but I don't think it has anything to do with the nomenclature I have coined (very much a Muñoz-Seca trait; my grandfather was an eminent playwright who loved to invent new uses for words).

[19] A colloquial term we used to define analyzing jobs and processes, where all the dirt present surfaces and is eradicated. More sophisticated names are lean or agile.

[20] A node with number of links.

Reinventing oneself as a high-level knowledge hub requires operational agility and flexibility to service the extended enterprise's whole ecosystem. Turning Pegasus into a hub required a very lean structure, one greatly equipped to solve novel problems and find solutions to issues that required investing in time. Curiously, in these situations the natural trend is to say "That's impossible," or "No can do". If there is something I have realized these past three years, it is that telling people "We don't do no" and "Service design makes the impossible possible" opens up totally unexplored horizons. It is what at Achilles, a firm belonging to a major bank, they call the "Think different" button. For them, viewing their efficiency program from a standpoint totally alien to the one they had used in previous restructuring programs made them understand the situation in a whole new light that has allowed them to design a novel and exhilarating comprehensive program for the whole company. Achilles will be a big player in the next chapter.

Summing up, there are three levels in the puzzle: the framework defined by the Promise, essence, flame red and the knowledge needed to implement the strategy; the individual pieces that have their operational structure; and the settings, or joining the pieces that fit into each other and having the glue to stick them together. And all that may sink into a very thick fog that will not allow the assembly to be seen clearly. What does fog lead to? Inefficiencies and service breaches that are so overwhelming that they do not allow the big picture to be seen.[21]

Smashing the *Muda*[22] to Lift the Fog that Gets in the Way of Seeing the Puzzle

The Pegasus CEO gave an order: "Time must be compressed." He specified his Promise by giving response time a score of 4/10 and margin 3/10. His essence was transparency and best practice. His flame red, their extended enterprise.

An exhaustive yearlong job allowed time-compressing actions to be determined. Curiously, many of the latter were not implemented at the time, since

---

[21] There is nothing I like more than a Monet painting. And they must be seen at a distance, from close up you see nothing. The same goes for Operations; the daily grind gets in the way of seeing the big picture.

[22] Wastage in Japanese. A great obsession among the Japanese. I am a big fan of the Toyota Production System (TPS) and all of its principles. Order and eradicating wastage is one of its mantras. Curiously, only a few of us get this, and actions like those that recently took place in the 2018 World Cup in Russia, where Japanese fans cleaned up the trash dumped by fans on the pitch, or their players clean up their changing rooms after them, should not surprise us, as this is indelibly stamped on their social behavior.

the organization blocked them.[23] Others, the obviously operational ones, were indeed implemented. The *muda* was so intense that only the obviously operational actions got resounding results. And the others? They had to get to work the following year on the service design for the organization to understand their scope, and as one of Pegasus's wonderful work group put it a couple of months beforehand[24]: "We do nothing but dust off actions they stopped us doing a year ago!" Now things were seen differently. Action was analyzed from the whole service design standpoint (Pegasus and its extended ecosystem) and the total impact of all of its elements was understood.

What shall we do, then, to tackle the *muda* of time, the big cancer in our companies? Juan, a Hephaestus manager in charge of the Emergency Department, was wondering just that. Hephaestus is a gas distribution company that sought to reinvent its service by partially applying SPDM considerations. The great impact of the extended enterprise on final customer satisfaction with the service made the CEO define his Promise as, "The extended enterprise must make my clients happy and stop suffering." His priority dimensions were timely reliability, with a score of 4/10 and response time, understood as running from any request to its response, with a score of 3/10.[25]

The service department had to be quick as well as reliable. But its manager was concerned, as he did not see his people working efficiently. However, when there was a gas emergency call, the response was like lightning, but there was a lot of time with no calls and that is where the lack of productivity was found.

He observed that one of the big problems arising was over interruptions, which were accepted as part and parcel of the daily routine. On the understanding that that was not acceptable, and it was intolerable that work should halt due to interruptions,[26] he drew up an action plan to bypass them.

What is the rationale behind downtime linked to interruptions? First, he sought to understand what the negative impact of an interruption consisted of. When somebody is interrupted, they have to start from scratch when getting back to work. Startup time is easy to measure for a machine, but not for brainpower. It varies greatly between people and jobs. Therefore, every time

---

[23] Pegasus is an unadulterated brainpower company. Making things happen means working hard to convince people that actions are wholly sound. And sound means different things to different people.

[24] I beg readers' indulgence for this emotional tone.

[25] Remember: reliability is one thing, time taken, another. I may be reliable with a response time of one year. I may be very quick and not at all reliable due to vagaries in my service.

[26] An endemic affliction in many companies.

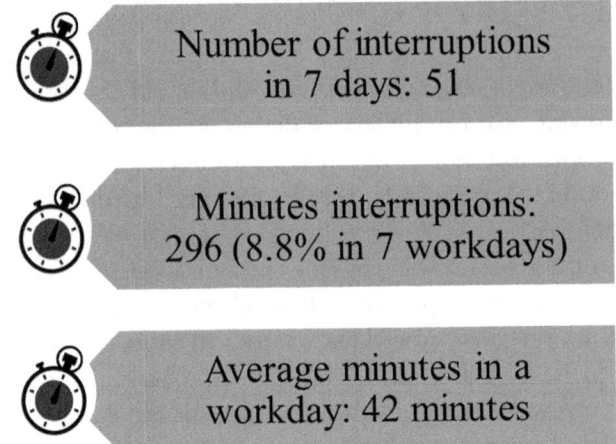

Number of interruptions
in 7 days: 51

Minutes interruptions:
296 (8.8% in 7 workdays)

Average minutes in a
workday: 42 minutes

Fig. 1.2 Juan's interruptions in a week's work

somebody is interrupted, the time for mental preparation must be added to the average time taken to do the ongoing job. And that increases the total time consumption.

Juan spent a week measuring downtime due to interruptions and spotting their causes. His aim was to understand in order to reduce them. Figure 1.2 shows the amounts of time consumed due to such interruptions.

Juan spotted a first type of interruption that he dubbed *social type*, which had nothing to do with work. A second type was in doing the job, but *due to misunderstanding of some process or task, that is not correctly determined. It stands apart from training plans, studies, regulations and so on, and is passed on by word of mouth. It is an informal type of knowledge that runs the risk of not being transmitted. A third type was those caused by queries over processes and tasks already implemented at the heart of the company. They will serve to detect training needs.*

Clearly the first type of interruption had to be eliminated. But Juan could not do that 100%, because it was not socially acceptable. He thought up a good solution: eliminate the interruption, but keep the social part. To do that, he proposed that his team should spend a few minutes at the start of each of the three shifts chatting about social/sporting events of the day, and then get to work. That action worked very positively.

Interruptions caused by the need to obtain informal knowledge that was not written down in codes and procedures were remedied by using an app that provided solutions to problems, and records of situations that had taken place. That enabled transmission between the three shifts and materialized knowledge for the company. Juan, who was this knowledge's main treasurer, generously dumped it into the app as it would free him from numerous interruptions.

The third type of interruption was remedied by a training program, which updated each of the three teams' knowledge.

Did interruptions disappear in this part of Hephaestus? Well no, but they were cut down drastically. Moreover, at the company level, the whole organization became aware of downtime due to interruptions and made an effort not to cause them.

Hephaestus's experience and spotting interruptions in other companies has led me to devise a classification of interruptions that I should like to share with readers. My classification of interruptions is divided into three categories: mess, laziness and knowledge gap.

- Interruption due to mess is caused by lack of operational efficiency. It is due to reprocesses, lack of specification of service components, queries over priorities or information breakdowns when taking decisions. All this can be fixed with a good operational efficiency plan. Querying the why to smash embedded actions that add no value, and analyzing the operational structure, allow the operating function to be overhauled.
- Laziness is allied to downtime. It is easier to ask somebody than seek the answer in codes or procedures. But let's not fool ourselves. Nobody, nobody, reads. Therefore, such interruption will not disappear until we devise abbreviated versions of codes of practice and procedures using audiovisual aids to speed up the learning curve. By making these tools available to the whole organization, we industrialize materializing knowledge and make it more efficient.
- Knowledge gaps cause interruptions but must not be solved this way. Managers must spot the type of problems agents face today and tomorrow and jointly design a knowledge acquisition plan. Tolerating this type of interruption does the company a disservice, as it clouds diagnosing the situation.

To see the Operations puzzle requires making time-wasting disappear throughout the operating system. Readers should not believe that mere lack of interruptions will lift the fog. But it is a usually poorly quantified element that I wished to share and that, in my experience with implementation these past years, greatly helps to rationalize operational efficiency. Of course, it greatly helped Juan to understand many of the deep-seated problems he had in his department.

Time compression at such junctures is a "hygienic" element in companies, and another driver in time-wasting is assigning brainpower the wrong jobs. Jobs must be assigned according to the knowledge stock agents have, or can develop using a gentle learning curve. It is as inefficient to have agents with a high knowledge stock doing low value-added jobs, as it is to have those with a low knowledge stock facing problems requiring greater knowledge. The outcome is the same: wastage, but the problem's cause is totally different.

Before entering into this distinction, allow me to retell something already mentioned in the preface, but that is now of greater import. Smashing *muda* and acting on operational efficiency requires understanding *that the mainstay of efficiency lies in appropriately using knowledge to solve service problems*. That central mainstay is often totally shrouded in layers of inefficiency, but when the latter are peeled off like the layers of an onion, it is revealed in its raw state. In the puzzle, we have located knowledge in a part of the framework to enable spotting whether the company has the stock needed to solve the problems it comes up against. But knowledge is likewise present in the operational pieces. Efficiency means solving problems nimbly after getting rid of all the *muda*.

Let us think for a moment. What is making things happen? Solving service problems[27] in the least possible time and thereby keeping the Promise made to the client. I may be oversimplifying, but at the end of the day, that's telling it like it is, isn't it? Depending on the strategy, problems will be heftier or simpler, but they are problems all the same. And problem equals solution. Therefore, being efficient means banishing wastage and applying the appropriate knowledge to solve problems.

Let us now return to the situation described two paragraphs above: inefficiency in using knowledge stock when matching it with the problem to be faced.

Pegasus gives us a good example of using brainpower with a high knowledge stock to do jobs that do not bring their potential productivity into play. One of Pegasus's critical knowledge cores lies in its Pricing area. The team was not satisfied with the response times it was providing the organization with and decided to understand the situation from the novel—for them—Operations standpoint. The great joy of working with smart people is that they learn quickly, and a fact-based analysis acquires all of its splendor. There is no need for emotional connotations; a fact is a fact and is overwhelming by

---

[27] Definition of "problem", according to the SPDM dictionary (Muñoz-Seca 2017): Situation that somebody finds unpleasant.

itself.[28] Looking at the tasks performed, it was soon noticed that a high percentage could be stripped from their daily duties. Some would be passed on to a standard back office, others to an "enlightened" back office, and a third category would be performed with the aid of technology. Such detailed analysis, which is explained here in a most cursory way, not only simplified jobs but essentially unlocked brainpower capacity to do the core jobs for their knowledge stock. Later on in the book we shall continue to explore that work, since it was very important in fixing Pegasus's response times.

Readers may now be wondering the following: And did these smart people not already get that? The answer is a blunt no. Very smart people, but at solving problems in their area of ability. And Operations are not often well known.

Now let us look at the other side of the coin. Brainpower having to do jobs for which they do not have the knowledge stock. Where is the inefficiency? Well it is simple. When a brain has no previous experience of a problem and cannot use an applicable solution process, it works by trial and error. In other words, by exploring. And that is value added for the company when the problem is new. But it is inefficiency if the problem is known to others, while that very brain does not have the knowledge. Coupled to that inefficiency there is defective management that has not been able to detect that knowledge gap. On many an occasion when I explain this in class, at the end a manager comes up to me and says: "I come to voice a *mea culpa* and tell you that you have just saved a colleague of mine's job." Delighted to have done so, but my operational concern is about inefficiency in using resources. Time-wasting is caused by something quite unnecessary for the company. Learning is of great value, but you need to spot what is not known and then learn. Solving by exploring to salvage a situation is a loss of efficiency for all involved. To sum up, wastage comes about when there is a mismatch between knowledge stock and the problem to be solved. Having a lot is just as inefficient as having little. And it all comes together as inefficient use of time.

Joining *muda* to time has been a big step forward for these companies in understanding how to improve their operational efficiency. Indirectly, it goes along with using knowledge and stresses the idea that effective implementation requires understanding how each agent uses their most precious belonging, time, in order to produce most effectively.

Lifting the fog to clearly see the puzzle requires, then, focusing on operational efficiency. Some of the key companies in this book have focused on

---

[28] Another sector where this goes on is medicine. Again, smart people facing empirical evidence (facts) are capable of solving problems that have arisen from antagonistic situations on a personal level. Another mantra of mine: let us work with facts, not opinions and much less with feelings.

response time as a critical element that does not allow them to look further. For that reason, they have worked on interruptions, time analysis and efficient use of knowledge. By remembering that problem equals knowledge, they have adjusted knowledge to problems and thus focused on efficiency.

The Operations puzzle enables understanding that operational strategy requires an overall view and cannot be undermined by focusing on inefficiency problems that arise like lava eruptions. Making things happen demands neatly spotting the action framework stemming from the strategy, in order to act on the three levels as determined.

SPDM Concepts Used in This Chapter

Chapters referred to: 2 and 3[29]

Based on the three SPDM levels (Fig. 1.3), the companies set off by spotting the first level comprising Promise, essence, flame red and knowledge stock.

The Promise (point I in the Conceptual Appendix), or strategy translation, has been broken down into five dimensions (point II in the Conceptual

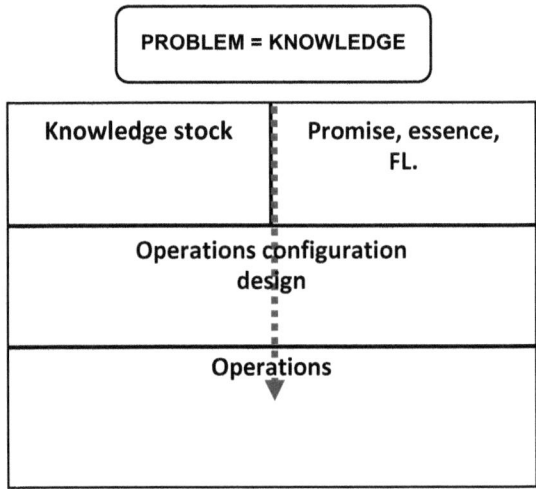

Fig. 1.3 SPDM conceptual blueprint

---

[29] The reference work is my previous book *How to Make Things Happen* (Muñoz-Seca 2017).

Appendix), and these have been prioritized (point III in the Conceptual Appendix) according to their importance in executing the strategy.

Essence is the company's DNA (point IV in the Conceptual Appendix). Essence may be joined to the company values and their symbiosis transformed into operational macro rules.

Flame red (point V in the Conceptual Appendix) has been described as that which sustains essence. Not detecting that may destroy it, leading to regrettable losses to a company's service.

We have defined problem equals solution. This definition enables operationalizing and materializing the knowledge needed to provide today's as well as tomorrow's service.

Finally, the service dream is senior management's (SM) wish materialized in a view of the future. Viewing that enables understanding the course SM wishes the service to take, and offers operational guidelines for every component in the organization.

Drawing up macro rules for Artemis's values and essence has introduced us to the 20 commandments (Muñoz-Seca 2017), a list of 20 basic rules drawn up to assist in implementing the Golden Triad. The Golden Triad seeks operational excellence through Efficiency, spawning learning or attractiveness and engaging the unit's agents.

The 20 Commandments

- Efficiency

1. We are the Yes Operations, not the No Operations
2. Make it simple, it will get complicated by itself.
3. The meaning of Operations: Why?
4. We don't want a $1-million improvement, but a thousand $1000 improvements
5. Everything may be queried until we agree
6. You must be "stuck to Operations"
7. You can only be managing director from 8:00 until 8:05 a.m.
8. You must be ready five minutes beforehand

- Attractiveness

9. Don't bring me problems, bring me solutions
10. Let's be aggressive and bold, but honest
11. Let's work on facts, not opinions
12. To make improvements work, all involved must end up winners (win-win)
13. To be world class takes talent and giving ground for it to show
14. A good manager must deliver letters

- Engagement

15. You must not do, but do-do
16. If you don't get there, I will
17. A good manager gets the best out of their people
18. We work, plural
19. To manage is to serve
20. To manage is to educate

SPDM is not easy to understand at first. For that reason, to make it easier to understand its conceptual synthesis, we suggest turning it into a picture of an Operations puzzle. This picture shows the three levels that comprise implementing the operational strategy, in a less academic way, so they may be easily absorbed. The puzzle applies to the company itself as well as the extended one. This concept will come along with us throughout the book, above all with Pegasus and Hephaestus, whose existence is based on the extended enterprise ecosystem.

Finally, this chapter has delved into a key aspect of inefficiency: interruptions. Preparation time has been analyzed as a key factor in brainpower interruptions.

Summing up, the initial main steps for implementing SPDM are as follows:

1. Starting with the strategy, sum up in a phrase what the company promises its clients. (Promise: Point I in the Conceptual Appendix).
2. The Promise is translated into criteria for the five dimensions (cost, time, range, innovation and consistency). Go dimension by dimension and enter each criterion's translation on the form (Point II in the Conceptual Appendix).
3. Prioritize the criteria: assign a score to each criterion. Scores must add up to ten points. Don't spread the scores out evenly; it will make the exercise unworkable. Assigning depends on how important each criterion is when keeping the Promise (point III in the Conceptual Appendix).
4. Now define the company's essence, its DNA (point IV in the Conceptual Appendix).
5. Next, spot the structure holding up the essence. That which makes the essence happen (point V in the Conceptual Appendix). That is its flame red.
6. Dream awhile. Depict how you would like to see your service's operational structure (point VI in the Conceptual Appendix).

7. Find the macro rules based on the scores and the 20 commandments.
8. Analyze your service ecosystem by thinking over the role the extended enterprise has in providing the service.

Chapter 1: Conceptual Appendix

I. The Promise

Promise	

II. Criteria for the Promise's dimensions

Dimension	Criterion (materializing the company dimension)
Cost	
Time	
Range	
Innovation	
Consistency	

III. Prioritizing criteria

Dimension	Criterion	Score
Cost		
Time		
Range		
Innovation		
Consistency		
Total		10

IV. The essence

Essence	

V. Flame red

Flame red	

VI. Service dream

Service dream	

2

No Hire, No Fire: Address Sustainable Efficiency Before Headcount

Abstract The motto "no hire, no fire" becomes an absolute must to make brainpower concentrate on value-added tasks that sustain their employability and the company's competitive edge. Our companies understand and act upon the need to address efficiency before they even consider getting new people on board. Technology becomes one of the great allies in freeing up brainpower from nonadded value tasks.

The Achilles CEO bluntly set out the situation facing him: "*Look*", he said, "*I want us to be the best in the world at what we do. I'm embarking on a very powerful Transformation Plan that means change using technology, realigning costs, incorporating new perimeters and much else besides. I need to use all the people I have, I need them to grow with me and scrap jobs that add no value, and get technology to do them instead. A transformation taken to mean firing some people to hire others is not my style. I want something different, to focus implementation on a plan and I believe SPDM can help us.*"

He had to make 700 people change their way of working and understand that technology, digital changes and all that went with that, was a wonderful opportunity.

Achilles had already done a lot of work on analyzing technology, rejigging processes and simplifying. The Transformation Plan was conceptually mature, as the specific software to be used, for example, had been chosen. SPDM would help as a vehicle for identifying possible gaps in issues that had not been analyzed, and drive implementation with engaging messages drafted as a challenge for the whole staff.

© The Author(s) 2019
B. Muñoz-Seca, *How to Get Things Right*, IESE Business Collection,
https://doi.org/10.1007/978-3-030-14088-5_2

This chapter focuses on Achilles. We shall meet the company again in other parts of the book, but this chapter deals with a group of its directors and managers that, for nine months, fought tooth and nail to show that an efficiency drive can be done by thinking of it as a change in value added, using a plan "of them, for them and by them".

What Must the Message Be?

Conceptually, the trial they were facing was the great challenge of the twenty-first century. I do not believe we should tolerate absurd apocalyptic notions abroad about technology and digitization. We face a wonderful opportunity; getting rid of jobs that add no value and getting technology to do them instead. Machines can do many things very well and humans should stop doing them. There are thousands of dull, repetitive jobs that can be done by machines. And not so dull ones, too. But let's start with the dull ones, which I call F5 jobs.[1]

The idea is obvious. Capacity is unlocked in agents doing F5 jobs, so they can move on to do greater value-added jobs that raise the company's contribution margin. It stems from the outlook that everybody in the company is an investment in know-how. It is neither feasible nor efficient to waste that. If capacity is unlocked, it is to perform new tasks. And for that they must learn how. Efficiency and productivity are imperative for survival. But not enough. Each company must be better at something, and for that it must use its capacity to create value-added, not F5, jobs.

The good thing about this message is its win-win focus. The company wins with more contribution margin, and the employee by taking on novel jobs that entails know-how. And such know-how cannot be taken away from them, and becomes their employability potential.

Figure 2.1 describes the link between all these components. The figure's mainstay is the need for operational efficiency so the core does not squander its resources. Getting there demands industrializing all that can be industrialized and using technology to do F5 jobs. That raises individual job output and unlocks capacity to take on new jobs with greater value added.

Obviously, hiring is unthinkable until everything falls into place. First seek efficiency by making resources produce more and better. Next, analyze whether the knowledge stock needed can be developed in house or new blood is required, due to time constraints or lack of basic structure.

A syllogism[2] suddenly came to me during a seminar at the IESE Munich, Germany, site, in the course of a long discussion with a Porsche AG manager:

---

[1] Key located at the top of the keyboard that refreshes the screen and folders.
[2] Reasoning formed by two premises and a conclusion that is the logical outcome of those premises. I formulate the two premises here, and the conclusion I leave to readers.

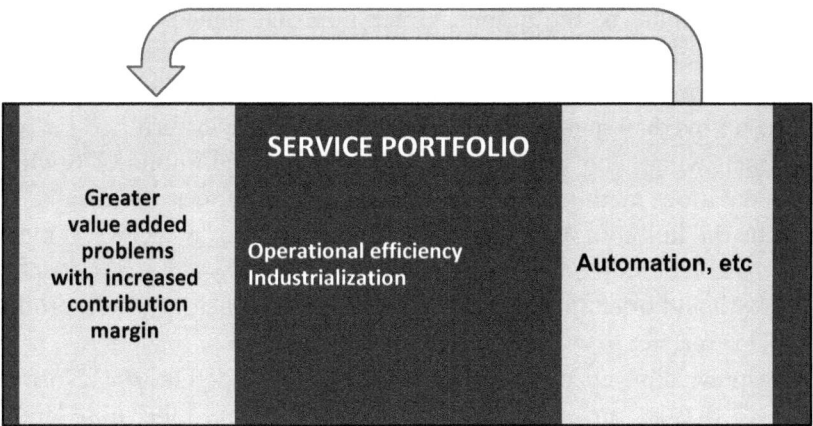

Fig. 2.1 The great opportunity

No hire, No fire.[3] It was the way to send a soothing message: until the whole structure was efficiently overhauled, nobody would be hired or fired. The idea struck home immediately and since then I have been using it as my main message for efficiency. Every company mentioned here uses it, and they have all confirmed that the message's beauty lies in its transparency. Brainpower requires practical and trustworthy messages, like this one.

What are the premises of No hire, No fire? First, cull efficiency by industrializing. Second, let technology and automation take off so that they can replace low-value jobs. Third, give humans higher value-added jobs that boost the company's contribution margin and provide them with new knowledge that will enhance their employability. Nothing is more valuable than to be prepared for new professional challenges, and brainpower is perfectly aware of the value added that entails. Therefore, No hire, No fire hinges on using knowledge, which is the force that transforms jobs. *Knowledge as problem-solving capacity*. Whether known or new problems. Let us delve into Achilles to see how to make those ideas happen.

G12 Is the Drive Behind Implementation

As a first step, Achilles set up a work group that for three years would act as watchdogs for implementing the Transformation Plan. The participants were several members of the board of directors, and some second-tier directors and managers. Representation was sought from every tier in the company and care was taken that participants were people that would bring "the voice of everyday

---

[3] Moreover, it is euphonious (pleasing to the ear), very much after the fashion of my ancestor…

reality" at Achilles to the group. A nice mix that signed a Non-disclosure Agreement (NDA) to keep the group sessions' deliberations under wraps.

They formed a group of 12 (dubbed G12) that worked for nine hard months on overhauling the plan. Each G12 member in turn had six people under their wing, who made up the G70. G12 would imbue G70 with the implementation methodology and critical issues under discussion. They would be the link to downward and upward messages, as each G70 member would have ten people under their wing that they would assess, brief, ask, debate with and brief on action to be taken. That capillarity would produce a trickle-down effect to every tier in Achilles.

That snowballing effect was designed in order to undertake the "Normandy landings", that is, implement the Transformation Plan. Like those landings, implementing the Plan had to be carefully studied and planned. There was no room for fits and starts, and attention to detail was important. A most important issue was predicting blocking factors that would arise, and the first one they spotted was vocabulary. G12 developed a list of cuss words that could not be used in any forum, as their connotations were very negative and brought back memories. Curiously, "efficiency" was one of them and it took some linguistic acrobatics to root it out.[4]

Following SPDM logic, the first conceptual task broached had to be the CEO defining Promise, essence and flame red. So it was, and that was shared in an interactive session with G12. Questions, clarifications and queries were broached in the meeting, which ended with fine-tuning the CEO's initial proposal.[5]

The Achilles Promise is to deliver the best quality at the best price with the guarantee of corporate supervision. Its priority dimensions are reliability (5/10), understood as timeliness and a low error rate; brainpower proposing improvements (3/10); and direct and indirect costs (2/10). Its essence is to be efficient, getting it right first time and its flame red what sustains knowledge and self-supervision of operational risk.

After that, G12 met weekly to design a three-year implementation plan by choosing some basic SPDM principles. As a G12 member put it in an email after a session held with G70: "Today has been very satisfying for me. I am sitting at home with a glass of wine in mission-accomplished mode." Effectively, the course had been plotted, staff were engaging with it and the initially set targets were being met. The landings had been a success. The first results could be seen. Let us look at some of the actions taken to get there.

---

[4] Undertaking a transformation plan for efficiency without using the term is somewhat suggestive.
[5] But the basic principles were stuck to. After all, the CEO owns the strategy and knows where the company has to go.

I-CAN

Achilles got the I-CAN project going to take aim at operational efficiency by spotting knowledge. "*I-CAN*", one of its proponents said, "*is about creating the momentum, the time and the obligation to think for ten weeks about my team's operational management, and about going over everything I do using a blank sheet of paper.*"

The work began with a pilot scheme that enabled learning and improved the way I-CAN was implemented. An important proposal consisted of some members of the pilot scheme acting as trainers/coordinators for implementing I-CAN in other areas.

The average duration of an I-CAN is 2.5 months, with weekly 1.5 to 2-hour meetings. Once the proposal to operate is done, its running is completely reviewed 90 days after implementation.

The I-CAN has become vitally important after nine months, and one of the Transformation Plan's cornerstones. Since then a prototype has led to nine finished I-CANs, and five that are nearly finished. Its success has been spreading like wildfire through every Achilles department, and there is a waiting list to deploy I-CAN in all of them.

I-CAN Pilot Scheme

Adriano, head of Fixed Income (G12 member), had a problem. He wanted to get his team on board with performing value-added tasks, but to do so he had to raise their efficiency and unlock capacity. Adriano literally absorbed SPDM concepts like a sponge, and has been a great cheerleader in deploying them.[6] A very creative person, he chose the SPDM concepts that suited him best to form his own I-CAN proposal. The pilot scheme started off from the problem = knowledge axiom[7] and focused on how to solve problems efficiently that the Achilles Fixed Income area came across.

I-CAN is built on the SPDM concepts listed in Fig. 2.2. Let us analyze the figure.

---

[6] This is very often the case with brains that sense they have an operational problem, but do not have the conceptual framework to really understand it and act. And when they are given the framework, they grasp it with untold strength and throw themselves into deploying it.

[7] And from the accepted definition that knowledge is the ability to solve problems.

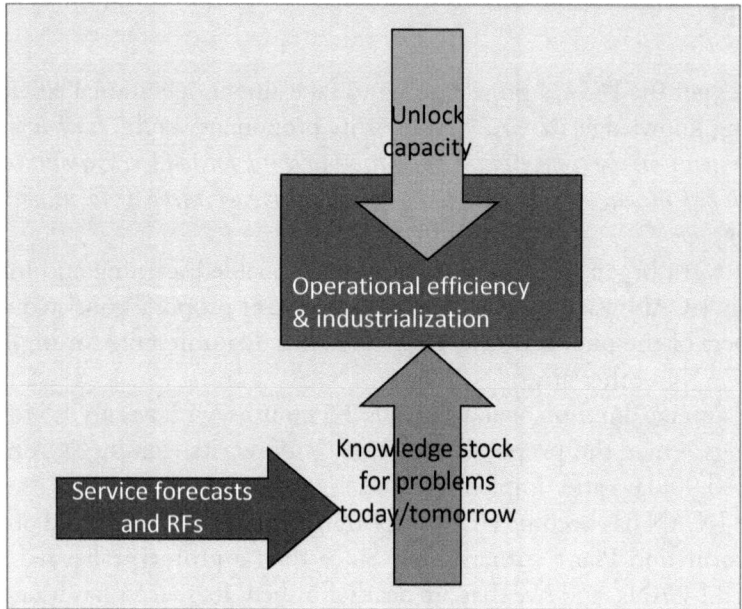

Fig. 2.2 SPDM primary objectives

- The upper arrow shows the need to unlock ability.[8]
- For that you must act on operational efficiency and industrialization. Technology is a component of operational efficiency and industrialization.
- The sideways arrow shows forecasts of, or needs for, knowledge that demand will bring. Knowledge to solve today's and tomorrow's problems. Forecasts should always come with adjustments (rolling forecasts) that make them certain.
- Knowledge stock is the mainstay for solving today's and tomorrow's problems. It is the basis for implanting sustainable efficiency.

Adrian mixed and matched these components to draw up I-CAN. Let us see how:

1. Adriano had noticed that his group acted a lot out of common sense. And everybody did things their own way, which made for scarcely efficient working. Operations rules would fix that, as they would steer prioritizing in his group. He defined an operational rule as *"encapsulated knowledge that provides guidelines and specifies priorities for their immediate use by*

---

[8] The following chapter deals with the concept of unlocking ability, so here we shall just mention it.

employees". As examples of operations rules, he indicated these two rules: "Day value deals have priority over future value deals," and "Within day value, those with platinum or high-value clients have priority over the rest."

Along with his team he spotted two types of rules at work: on the one hand, those used informally and widely known; on the other, those that were formalized, as they had been spotted in specifying the service agreed with the client. One goal was to formalize the informal[9] rules so that they would be known to the whole team, not just a few.

I-CAN 1: Defining operations rules

2. The focus then shifted to understanding demand. For that, problems were classified according to the reasoning that defined them. In I-CAN, a problem is defined as "various situations in a process that require an action to be solved". One problem was classified as "Spanish market settlement", or "Italian market settlement", or "American market settlement".

I-CAN 2: Classifying problems

3. As per problem = knowledge, the next step is spotting the knowledge stock needed to solve the type of problems arising. By spotting problems whose solution is known, we can cull the knowledge available to solve them. The Achilles G12 agreed that problem = task = knowledge. Therefore, the level of dismantling knowledge at Achilles lay in the task being performed.[10] Culled knowledge is initially categorized in the five SPDM layers of knowledge. Nonetheless, once the prototype had been set up, it was found that the numerical terminology led to undesired comparisons[11] that unsettled the group. Therefore, the Roman numerals I to V were changed to letters

---

[9] Obviously, after analyzing whether they are right. At times, informal rules are right for a small group, but not for the service in general. And that may not be formalized. Only what adds value to providing the service may be formalized. The rest must be overhauled.

[10] In the next chapter, when we delve deeper into primary and secondary tasks, we shall see how Hephaestus wanted to unbundle knowledge types in as much detail as possible. Depending on each company's taste. What is important is their use in improving efficiency.

[11] From "I know more and you less", and all of us must know a lot. Completely wrong. The right level is needed to tackle the problem arising.

A to E. This removed comparisons and focused the level on the real knowledge needed to solve the problem.

I-CAN 3: Spotting knowledge and its level

---

4. Planning and rolling forecasts are essential elements in I-CAN. Adriano planned once a week, on Friday afternoons, bearing in mind what people would be around the following week. That way he could match the flow of problems that would come his way the following week, with the knowledge stock held by the people he would have available.[12] That allowed him to forecast possible problems that would crop up and adapt the service to incoming demand.

Furthermore, every morning a supervisor would make a rolling forecast to adjust initial forecasts to the passage of time. Every day, incoming demand may vary as well as people available to tackle incoming problems.[13] Variations inherent in Fixed Income demand make it indispensable to thus adjust actual incoming problems, to the knowledge stock available on each particular day.

I-CAN 4: Planning and rolling forecasts

---

5. Incoming tasks at Fixed Income may be separated into primary and secondary tasks. Primary tasks are those that require immediate attention and a zero-minute response time. For example, "present-day value" deals in Fixed Income. Secondary tasks are those that can be organized and planned for whenever it suits the agent.

Once the Fixed Income prototype was tested, "primaries"[14] were redefined as those that must be performed "intraday by 4 p.m.", that is, by market close. After market close at 4 p.m., there is no longer any rush. The task is then an

---

[12] Readers should note that knowledge stock is matched, not people. I may have physical people, but not the knowledge stock needed to solve the problems that come my way.

[13] Unexpected absences, for example.

[14] When a task is primary and when secondary may be defined in each company according to its Promise and circumstances. The basic idea is: "primary", immediate response time (zero minutes). The rest, "secondaries".

aborted deal and it makes no difference whether it is done at 6 p.m. or 8 p.m. It is thus a secondary task and how it best matches brainpower may be planned for.

6. Operational efficiency must go hand in hand with fulfilling the service and following preventive measures. Achilles' Promise specifies reliability as a total priority. Thus, I-CAN entails finding preventive indicators in order to achieve that. Indicators must prevent failure. Crying over service breaches is not efficient. In services, you must act five minutes ahead. Identifying possible failures that might crop up is sustainable, and for that indicators are required to help spot the risk elements. And to act preventively.

I-CAN distinguished between two types of indicator: those that reveal everyday work and enable following it up quantitatively, and those that assess the level of service provided. The former would act as an early warning to prevent breaches in the latter. An example of a service level indicator is, "Having no breach due to Achilles for more than 30 days". And a preventive indicator is, "Following up mismatched breaches daily."

7. The list of knowledge types that arise in I-CAN may be woven into Achilles' services portfolio. Said portfolio is now composed of tasks and services. The next step is to structure the portfolio by knowledge types, since that makes for more flexibility when mixing them. I-CAN is a first step toward achieving that. I-CAN knowledge types may act likewise as a basis for other actions in the Achilles Transformation Plan. On the one hand, in the New Services Specification that we shall see in Chap. 4. On the other, to determine the Achilles knowledge map that allows resources to be assigned to new demands or perimeters[15]:

---

[15] As we shall see in Chap. 6.

These seven components comprise the methodology that Achilles designed. But group work did not stop there. A methodological mini group comprising Adriano and the leading I-CAN coordinators drew up some lessons learned and to be pooled with the new crews of I-CAN coordinators. "We pooled all we had learned so that they do not start from scratch and take away a minimum of knowledge types, which are those that the more senior coordinators have already dealt with. The idea came to the first three of us coordinators."

Considerations, and lessons learned and spotted, are the following:

- I-CAN is about wondering whether things can be done differently. It is not about querying the department head's management style. It is not about chasing up what is done badly. We are interested in knowing whether things can be done differently.
- Every meeting clearly spots one or two deliverables. The head of I-CAN convenes weekly meetings at the beginning of the period.
- The I-CAN calendar is drawn up and agreed to in the first work session. The plan's progress will be determined by whether agreed deadlines are met.
- Each I-CAN's owner is the area head. The coordinator's role is that of driver/contrast/coach/guide. His job is done before the weekly work group meeting coordinated by the area head.
- In each weekly session, the area head is free to incorporate such people from his group as he deems fit. It is better not to incorporate the area head's manager into the weekly meetings so as to ensure that area head performs a creative realignment exercise, by obtaining help from the work group's other members.
- The work group is emailed weekly with a report on each of the seven components launched by the I-CAN plan and a summary of agreements reached, the session's deliberations and a to-do list for the next weekly session. The area manager is cc'd on the report.
- The project managers periodically receive a report on the percentage of progress achieved versus forecasts. Moreover, an indicator will warn of any departure from the timetable planned and agreed with the head.
- Ninety days after finally implementing I-CAN (I-CAN Certification), the new management model is completely reviewed. In some cases, a second review is needed three months later in order to meet a higher industrialization target.
- When the I-CAN is done, the project head must hand the area director an estimate of how much capacity has been unlocked by industrializing (by eliminating, merging and reviewing tasks or by reorganizing operations) and has yet to be done (automation, robotics, etc.).

- The groups themselves must reach the conclusions. Each one will work at their own pace and several iterations may be needed. The presence of outsiders in a group will breathe fresh air into such vices as they may have already acquired.

To follow up this learning process, the I-CAN coordinators meet for a weekly work session (30/60 minutes) to share methodological and learning issues. In those meetings, coordinators table what they have found to be new and significant that week, the blockages and difficulties coordinators come across when working with other I-CAN groups, or following laggard or more complicated I-CANs, or whatever might be causing the complication.

I-CAN has developed two functions: the area coordinator that manages the process of diagnosing, analyzing and realigning tasks, and the one we have introduced in the last few paragraphs. And the *methodological driver* that looks after and supports implementing I-CAN methodology. Adriano devised this function on the basis that coordinators needed continual coaching and that I-CAN needed drivers to ensure that it was correctly implemented. Cross-fertilizing and pollinating problems and lessons between both groups lead to significant preventive wealth.

The Achilles G12 made an important point about the impact of I-CAN and what was learned in the months they have been implementing it. As an example, there is the inception of the Efficiency Unit. That unit, under the CFO's wing, receives structural adaptations undertaken once I-CAN has finished and shares out remaining capacity to the rest of Achilles. The criterion for delivery is available capacity added to the knowledge needed to perform today's and tomorrow's tasks[16] coupled with future forecasts. Help from HR is indispensable for this linkage and the need for it to take part in the whole Transformation Plan is evident.

From a Prototype to a Way of Operating

The transformation from a prototype to a stable way of operating is a road paved with learning. The I-CAN methodological drivers' team has summed up the ten principles of the I-CAN way.

1. **Act five minutes ahead.** The I-CAN methodological drivers set up a forum for sharing lessons learned from the implementation process in order to prevent problems and share positive as well as negative experiences. It consists of 45-minute meetings, no phones or computers.

---

[16] We shall look more deeply into that in Chap. 6.

2. **Active learning.** Polish the methodological drivers' methodology using lessons learned and by industrializing knowledge.
3. **Use the analysis done to cull all of its potential.** Spot inefficiency, industrialize wherever possible and spot F5 jobs that a robot can do, when performing the task analysis.
4. **An opportunity to look out for number one.** The methodological driver, as a lever for spotting the potential focus of what impact the exercise may have on improving participants' workaday lives. The opportunity enables restructuring tasks and organizing to make them more efficient, and for the latter to follow through to best practice by participants: for example, less overtime, less Saturdays, more structured work and KISS.
5. **Tempo.** Freedom for each I-CAN to take the time they deem fit, as coordinators set the pace (or the orchestra conductor's tempo when conducting a piece of music).
6. **Mental model.** Participants incorporate the mental model that they will use once the I-CAN exercise is done. Absorbing the method is the result of incorporating the way to go using the good results obtained.
7. **A space for sharing upsets.** I-CAN is then an escape valve for sharing daily upsets and focusing on them as blockages the I-CAN project must get rid of. Starting from scratch allows work areas to be jointly spotted where I-CAN can help smash inefficiency.
8. **Out of the box.** Encourage exploratory creativity[17] by bringing a colleague from another area to the group, one that although aware of what is done in the area and can offer a totally different view of problems. It is the technique of looking through "different spectacles" at problems in order to cull hitherto unimaginable solutions.
9. **Autoritas.** Choosing the methodological drivers based on their personal *autoritas*. The drivers must be capable of hauling and the authority to do so can be earned only by best practice.
10. **Proactive querying.** The drivers must likewise have a personal history of pushing for proactive querying.[18] Following the Toyota Production System (TPS) principles, query everything, be unsettled and curious, and spark improvement.

---

[17] There are various types of creativity (Boden 1991). The combinatory type is the simplest, the exploratory type arises in the exploration process, and the transformation type breaks molds.

[18] Some of them call it being brazen (dictionary definition: brazen, defiant, insolent, disrespectful), and I take it to mean defiant.

The Difference Between Don't Know and Don't Want

Along with I-CAN, Achilles developed a complementary project focused on spotting knowledge gaps and the existing knowledge stock. G12 defined it as a project "to set up a freely accessible repository for documentation of our projects that reinforces our knowledge, streamlines learning and is available to any employee".

The project was launched when G12 found that Achilles had a great deal of knowledge encapsulated informally, but of whose existence only a few were aware. Notepads full of information for third parties to use crisscrossed the company without anyone spotting what a "treasure" they were. Such know-how had to be materialized and shared around, as the risk of losing it was very high indeed.

"TREASURE" had the aim of spotting, sharing, assessing and improving existing knowledge at Achilles. Its focus is: "*We are all indispensable at the level of promised service and we can all improve. We must share.*"

Once I-CAN is done and the group's real knowledge spotted, TREASURE gets going to spot *what agent performs tasks in the least time consumed while sticking to the promised service.* Finding who solves problems most efficiently sets the benchmark for others to follow.

The baseline hypothesis is that the benchmark is set because that agent has differential knowledge that allows them to solve the problem much more efficiently. Achilles had spotted that some agents' know-how was not shared around. This means there were agents that treated problems as if they were nearly new when another agent had already solved them many times. They invented what had already been invented. The conceptual idea is that the process of solving problems with something known (applicative) cannot consume as much times as when it is new. And spending time on finding something that is not new is inefficiency. To enhance efficiency, TREASURE focused on materializing and sharing knowledge.

TREASURE is then set, and works, in four steps:

1. Spot the process's criticality.
2. Gather and classify the process's documentation.
3. Certify usefulness.
4. Self-assessment/self-management to enable improvement and individual learning.

1. *Spot the process's criticality.* As a first step, spot the process to be used. The selection criterion is what adds most value to delivering the service. For that, use I-CAN as a basis for analyzing priority and its volumetrics. Once selected, knowledge is culled from it.[19]

2. *Gather and classify documentation* of prioritized processes. Once the knowledge has been spotted, all the relevant documentation must be gathered together. One must ponder whether all the informal documentation[20] needs to be materialized to thus complete the process.[21] Documentation is classified according to its contents and connection to other processes (hashtags and comments). To streamline the search, each document must have a brief synopsis. Indexing must follow the SPDM verb, object, condition (VOC) format that identifies documents and streamlines the search for them in the platform where they are stored. Documentation must be on paper or in video form. TREASURE prefers video as the standard format, since videos[22] are easy to make, nimble and graphic. Nowadays, any platform supports videos and they make it easy to share knowledge.

The documents' contents must be summarized in the *knowledge pill*[23] format. A pill contains the knowledge needed to solve a specific and focused problem. There are two types of pill: formative and informative.

- *Training pills* aim to streamline learning or transmit knowledge. For example, if a video is made where an expert explains how to modify a particular detail in a fixed-income issue, its synopsis and indexing might be as follows (Table 2.1):

Table 2.1 VOC example in TREASURE

Synopsis	VOC		
	Object	Verb	Condition
Explanatory document for modifying the pool factor in a fixed-income issue	*Pool factor*	Modify	System A
	Bonds	*Set up*	System B
	Fixed income		System C
	FI		
	Bond		
	Fixed income		

---

[19] This chapter's conceptual appendix contains the SPDM forms for doing this.

[20] Documentation found in individual computers, post-its, and so on. It is usually a lot and often very important.

[21] E2E, end to end.

[22] Videos must be no more than two minutes long.

[23] We shall look more closely at pills in Chap. 6.

- *Information* pills: do not go into detail for specific tasks to solve specific problems. They contain information relevant to the latter. For example, what is a bond? What is a commodity?

3. *Certifying usefulness* of documents and videos. TREASURE is 95% focused on videos, as they are very attractive and easy to use. Certification consists in checking that contents help solve tasks (problems), and are validated and certified to prove their usefulness. This is checked by making sure that an agent with little knowledge can perform the task using the documentation provided (video or written).

4. *Self-assessment* of knowledge coupled with *self-management* in performing tasks to *improve learning*. This point caused a bit of a stir at Achilles, as it tampered with a certain tendency to point fingers. Drawing on a basic TPS principle that envisages learning by self-assessment, TREASURE favors assigning incidents to the people causing them, so they might learn from them. This goes along with calling periodic meetings to review incidents arising to analyze their root cause. It is all about learning and improving, the age of finger-pointing is over.

TREASURE started with two prototypes and has been completed in three areas, with another seven under way. TREASURE has become a cornerstone in developing the knowledge stock Achilles requires. Likewise, the knowledge industrialization plan allows easy access to solutions for problems that have already been solved.

TREASURE comes into play in Achilles' operations culture. It provides real implementation of the following: "More is learned from a mistake than something done well." The person making the mistake is the one that solves it, and thus improves. The mantra "A mistake enables learning" is well known, but difficult to implement in bossy environments. Therefore, TREASURE stresses not pointing fingers and is based on showing that a mistake may be a symptom.

A Symptom of What? Don't Know or Don't Want to?

Distinguishing between the two is important. Don't know is not the same as don't want to. It does not call for the same action. If somebody does not know, they are introduced to TREASURE. If somebody does not want to, they are given three opportunities. Please, dear reader, don't confuse the symptoms. Make sure your people know, but do not want to, before playing the three-opportunities card. Multiple times an attitude that seems to convey "Don't want to" is really fear of saying, "Don't know." Talking to their immediate superior helps to understand the reason behind the refusal. Nobody can pass up an opportunity to learn.

Taken from scripture, the three opportunities are chances given to a worker to sail in the transformation ship. The ship sets sail, and sails with or without them. What ship each person sails on is an individual decision.

What are the three opportunities? The boss gives the first opportunity, the boss's boss the second, and HR the third, or whoever performs that function at the company. The chance to learn is offered in all three, the reasoning behind the need to transform is explained to them, the why and wherefore, and the important role everybody plays. But if they reject all three opportunities, then for all that this chapter is entitled No hire, No fire that brain does not belong on this particular ship.

No hire, No fire places efficiency and unlocking capacity before hiring, but we cannot accept dysfunctional attitudes. Therefore, the sooner and clearer, the better. They will surely find new horizons to suit them. Brainpower is wayward when operating and a clear line of action must be defined. Transparency, consistency and clarity must always be used with them. But the CEO sets the course, and if it does not suit them, then they must seek pastures anew. Telling it like it is. There is no time, action is an immediate necessity.

Achilles has adopted this approach and G12 has clearly conveyed it to the 70. The rules of the game are fixed.[24] Anybody that does not like them must look for some other ship.

SPDM Made to Measure: Allowing Freedom to Adapt

SPDM focuses on efficiency and sustainability using a few steps. But it must not prevent creativity and adaptability from emerging in groups. Thus, we have seen Adriano set up his I-CAN, and TREASURE adopting indexed knowledge. And both using knowledge as the cornerstone of efficiency.

---

[24] That does not mean implementing them will be easy. It takes a lot of determination to see it through and people falter. It is a change in operating culture that must be consolidated and that, always, takes perseverance, constancy and backing from senior management.

But one of the work subgroups went a step further in doing so its own way. Its director was decisive for that. Somebody totally devoted to supporting their people in the revamp, but a very independent thinker that composed place and method himself.[25]

He did not want to wholly accept already-tested prototypes.[26] With I-CAN he cherry-picked what appealed most to him. Same with TREASURE. This director stuck to the music and wrote his own score. The trouble is that, at times, musical approaches do not consider crucial components like service design, and become short-sighted. They concentrate on the level of efficiency and miss the chance to go the extra mile. But they have to see the big picture themselves, bit by bit. There is nothing worse than pushing brainpower around. They must be shown the way and given the tools for the job, and must discover horizons themselves.

As described in the following text box, the "musical" group focuses on operational efficiency based mainly on the 4W & H. This is a most useful tool that allows all inefficiency to surface and drives industrialization.

Efficiency

- Consider what is sought after

  - Redesigning an overall process
  - Take an everyday task, broaden the view and redesign it

- What for

  - Reduce incidents
  - Unlock capacity and boost efficiency
  - Improve service levels, improve our job

- How

  - Plot a beginning and end
  - Draw the As Is
  - Analyze, study and propose improvements
  - Design the To Be

- What we get

  - Take on more jobs while staying the same
  - Chance to simplify processes
  - We win, the bank wins

---

[25] Every company has them. There is no need to confront them; they must be managed and engaged. They are smart and contribute. And always, at some stage, they realize what they are missing. Perseverance and patience is the way to deal with them.

[26] They never say NO. They always seek twists and turns and must be allowed to wander.

But when the music stops and nobody knows how to carry on, other inspiration must be found. As we shall see in Chap. 8, this group has explored new pathways. Along with other G12 areas, it has cocreated an approach to improvement that other groups are using. The joint work has broadened outlooks and added SPDM concepts in order to query elements that had not been analyzed. Starting with its own musical contribution, it has received in-house backing to compose a symphony. This director holds the "No hire, No fire" principle sacred, and the great job he has done with two other G12 members and his own team has realigned and grown its own resources.

Finally, G12 itself picked some SPDM issues and left out others. It did not find them relevant to the challenge facing them. The following text box summarizes some of the issues Achilles embraced heartily and adds the finishing touch to this chapter.

Agreements Reached by Achilles in Its Transformation Plan Inspired by SPDM

1. The Plan's mainstay is cutting consumption in order to unlock capacity and apply it to greater value-added services.
2. The big mainstay for industrialization is knowledge stock.
3. Incorporating aggregate planning, scheduling and rolling forecasts as keys to industrialization.
4. Using as a baseline for each project the best agent's average and long-term execution time (while meeting specifications).
5. Approaching implementation by using quick wins and pointing out successes to learn from them, and ramp up implementation.
6. An action plan to get everybody on board, albeit at different speeds.

- Same message
- Same vocabulary
- Same aim

7. The list of cuss words is a group of words to avoid when implementing the Transformation Plan.
8. Key performance indicator (KPI):

- Unlocked capacity (measured by full time equivalent (FTE))
- Increase in input (measured by FTE)
- Eight families for grouping preventive indicators.

SPDM Concepts Used in This Chapter

Chapters referred to: 5

This chapter's mainstay is using knowledge to achieve efficiency. SPDM deems knowledge to be problem-solving capacity. And that is the sole meaning we shall use. Knowledge is a most complex issue that is not up for debate here. In the operations approach, all that matters is whether we know how to solve incoming problems today and tomorrow. Period. Nothing else. Therefore, problem = knowledge (point I in the Conceptual Appendix). This is how we use it and this is what we call it. In this chapter, Achilles decided that problem = task = knowledge. That's a simple way to deal with it.

Likewise, we must spot the knowledge level that we have and need. SPDM spots five knowledge levels

1. *Know about (KA)*: The subject has information about the state of a particular knowledge type.
2. *Know-how (KH)*: The subject has skills that enable the procedural use of knowledge.
3. *Know why (KW)*: The subject is able to understand the fundamental logic of the knowledge type and think about it.
4. *Know-how to improve (KI)*: The subject has the knowledge level needed to solve problems relating to change and progress. The subject can extend knowledge and modify its use.
5. *Know-how to learn (KL)*: The subject can modify the fundamental logic of the knowledge type and is capable of self-learning. This knowledge type brings about a change in the subject's mental structure and drives their capacity to learn.

How to get knowledge is another relevant issue in the chapter. Adults get knowledge by learning. And you get learning by solving problems. Therefore, you get knowledge by solving problems.

When a problem is known, adults apply solutions already known to them. When a problem is new, adults must create knowledge by exploring, by trial and error. Exploring takes time, but it gets fresh knowledge. Applying is swift, but does not spawn fresh knowledge (or spawns very little). Investing time in solving known problems by exploring means a great loss in efficiency. Therefore, materializing knowledge is critical.

Getting a knowledge list means indexing it simply. For that, the SPDM indexing format, verb, object, condition (VOC) may be used (point II in the Conceptual Appendix).

Verb: a transitive verb implying action on a recipient.
Object: The recipient of the action indicated. The action modifies this object in some way.
Condition: Complementary conditions that must enable solving a problem.

Problems or knowledge types have an inflow. This inflow may be forecast and for that it is worthwhile planning for incoming problems. Planning demand for problems follows the same principles as planning for product demand. SPDM makes problems tangible and materializes them as if they were production items. Materializing them means we must treat knowledge as something almost physical that follows the same productive principles as stocks. Therefore, we call it knowledge stock.

Finally, the chapter deals with operations rules (point III in the Conceptual Appendix). A rule is encapsulated—or materialized—knowledge to convey a way of operating. Rules may be macro rules like those we saw at Artemis in the previous chapter, or operations rules as defined by Adriano. Operations rules help decision-making and allow people to be clear about management priorities. Operations will always be about deciding and if prioritizing is not made clear, it will be done by common sense. And decisions based on common sense are usually bad for keeping the company Promise.

Operations rules may be formal or informal. Informal ones arise from informally solving problems; nobody has materialized them and they are stored in individual brains.

Chapter 2: Conceptual Appendix

I. Spotting knowledge

Knowledge spotted in problems	
Problem	Associated knowledge that solves it

II. VOC

Verb	Object	Conditions	Comments
Acting on a recipient (verbalizing knowledge)	The action's recipient	Complementary conditions that a problem must meet (categories, time constraints, etc.)	Comments that will help understand knowledge

What do I know?	What level do I have?	What do I need to solve problems?	Source
Knowledge in VOC format	*From I to V*	*VOC from I to V*	*Who has the knowledge?*
Knowledge 1			
Knowledge 2			
Knowledge 3			

III. Operations rules

	Formal	Informal
Rules		

3

Unlocking Capacity to Tackle Higher Value-Added Tasks

Abstract Capacity analysis allows all our brainpower to be aware of how they perform their tasks, the time they consume in each one, and provides benchmarks in the form of efficient problem-solving agents. The challenge is to find optimal consumption and learn from it. Based mainly on two of our companies, the chapter shows how to perform a capacity analysis matrix and reveals the added value results that the companies achieved.

Any improvement action must start out by considering a capacity analysis. There is no point in trying to seek efficiency and improvement without having really diagnosed what your people spend their time on. Therefore, capacity analysis has been at the start of each action by the four companies featured in this book.[1] Knowing what you spend your time on, how you spend it, why you spend it and how you use it, are absolutely critical to determining both individual and company efficiency. Time fritters away and is very easy to waste.[2]

There is beauty in all this time-compression approach to operational efficiency. It is enough to become aware of its fleeting quality to immediately take measures to improve. When I introduced brainpower at Pegasus to the seven-times concept,[3] and the importance of understanding how operations time is

---

[1] Achilles, to a lesser extent, as it has already performed nonindividual capacity analyses. It works in progress that must be done.

[2] Personally, I favor wasting time while on vacation. I think it is very healthy, because the mind must also relax. I always say that watching grass grow is one of my favorite hobbies while on vacation, when I get the chance.

[3] Remember (and if you do not, look at the end of the chapter): seven times: operation, preparation, batch, queue or interference, planning, safety and disruption.

© The Author(s) 2019
B. Muñoz-Seca, *How to Get Things Right*, IESE Business Collection,
https://doi.org/10.1007/978-3-030-14088-5_3

value-added time, I began to hear comments like "This elevator has a huge preparation time and for me it is downtime" and "I will plan my visits knowing where I will park, because time spent looking for a lot is worthless." And understanding the importance of efficiency when starting meetings on time, and ditto for ending them. All a waste of time and rife in Pegasus, and possibly in many other companies.[4]

When starting on any quest for efficiency, a mental outline must be transmitted to the brainpower to make them understand the whys and wherefores. Capacity analysis involves wading into analyzing tasks, time consumption, incoming demand, delays, queues and waiting times. It all adds up to a new way of looking at the world around you, and understanding that what matters is not being there, but producing.[5] You can be there less hours yet produce more. This is a win-win situation for everybody, ecological balance included.[6]

> The first indispensable step for making things happen is to share with brainpower a mental model to make them see the evidence of their daily lack of productivity.

This step entails banishing the idea that everybody is super- or overworked and has no time for anything. Let alone for thought and analysis.[7] This is not so. What everybody is doing is wasting time and working inefficiently. Therefore the overactivity bubble must be burst by analyzing time consumed by each agent. Each of our companies did so and the outcome has been, as ever, very positive. Not only is time spent on each job compressed, but the idea is grasped that time slips "between the cracks".

Finding Consumption

Hephaestus, as you would expect in a gas company, has an Emergency Department. Emergency immediately tackles any problem related to gas leaks, among other important issues for the welfare of the general population.

---

[4] Clearly I am being prudent. In every company I go to, I see time wasted left and right.

[5] Several pupils of mine have told me that in their companies outside Spain, if you stay late at work, they come to ask you if anything is wrong. Or turn out the lights to make you leave. I think that is how it should be, as long as the time spent at work has been productive.

[6] Among others, less electricity consumed by compressing time for heating, air conditioning, lighting and so on.

[7] It seems everybody wants to do things. Thought and diagnosis are not sexy. And we squander huge resources doing things that are then of little use, but the main thing is to do them. Big mistake!

The Emergency director wanted to focus on capacity utilization among members of the three shifts. He wanted empirical proof that it was well dimensioned, and to prevent possible problems in future. The delicate nature of the service demands it.

The head of the Emergency Unit, Pedro, told his group that they would all tackle the exercise between them. They had to understand what they spent their time on in order to rationalize its use and, above all, to make their jobs more efficient and effective. Starting with the "No Hire, No fire" principle, the director as well as Pedro sought to engage the Emergency group in the job.[8]

The components' first reaction was as expected: "We have no time for anything and our occupancy rate is very high." No surprise there, it is the standard response.

The way to go is to sit the group down and work with them on the consumption details. A capacity analysis always results in very high occupancy rates, at first. That result arises because the consumption analysis is usually done badly. Thinking of a job's average consumption is somewhat difficult and takes some training. The first exercise must therefore always be approximate for the terms of the analysis to become familiar, and for the structure to take root in a processor's mental model. High variability in services is a very important factor, and what is really critical is that processors should understand the capacities' dynamics, so they may constantly assess themselves on time used in their jobs.

From that moment on, the "I need more people" mantra should disappear as it must turn into "I have very high occupancy and we need to see how we can industrialize and use technology to compress consumption." If, once this aim has been achieved, resources really are not enough, then capacity will have to be sought by incorporating resources in-house or from the extended enterprise.

> The capacity analysis mechanics allow a new idiom to be developed, where time consumption becomes the mainstay of acting and no new hires are foreseen until consumption has been perfectly industrialized and weighed up.

The Hephaestus Emergency group analyzed the processes they performed and classified the tasks by groups, in order to simplify the analysis. Thus some groups were dubbed home notification management, grid notification management, planned work management, fraud management, third-party damage management, dispatching alarms management, grid action log, emissions delivery reports or monitoring working equipment.

---

[8] Engaging is important because the one that knows best how to improve things is the one that does them. Without engaging each and every agent, it is almost impossible to find ways to improve. TPS principles again.

When drawing up these groups, it was noticed immediately that the first two had a very important element: they required immediate response, without delay. Zero-minute response time. Clearly, an emergency call of this type is a primary task. The rest may be organized and planned for. All other tasks are therefore secondary.

The group took a drastic turn when it was presented with that concept of primary and secondary activities. The director made them see that their principal and primary activity was serving clients in emergencies. When questioned whether this could mean that each one's occupancy time could be very low on average, the answer was a resounding YES. And that is how it should be. Emergency demand cannot be planned for, so there is a lot of randomization and this group's average and long-term occupancy rate for such activities must be low. The Promise makes that obligatory.

> Distinguishing between primary and secondary activities allows capacity usage to be reorganized so as to act more assertively on the service's Promise.

Once primary and secondary tasks have been spotted, the Emergency Department threw itself into understanding job consumption. The first time somebody faces consumption, they mix up concepts and get confused. Thus we have to be very clear. Consumption must be counted by task type and long-term average (LTA). Meaning what is spent on average on doing a task. Just one. And on average. Averages may be worked out from one week's observations. Or approximate averages. Everything may be refined and refined.

At Hephaestus Emergency, they compiled one month's data. And worked out averages. The resulting figures showed that coordinator 1 for the "home notification management" task group had an LTA consumption of 0.25 hours. And that same coordinator had an LTA consumption of 4 hours for "grid notification management" (Fig. 3.1). These consumption figures are the ones to use when analyzing occupancy rates for components' primary tasks in the Emergency Unit (Fig. 3.1).

This consumption figure means that in one hour (60 minutes) an LTA of four home emergency calls may be taken (0.25 hours, i.e. 15 minutes). And that the coordinator consumes four hours on grid management; thus, two calls per day can be taken (in an eight-hour day). Obviously, the first thing the group wondered was whether the consumption figures could be lowered.[9]

---

[9] It is always the first thing to wonder once the consumption figures are there.

MORNING SHIFT	FTE	NUM BER	UNIT CAPACITY hours/hours	TOTAL CAPACITY	Home alerts management (MAIN)	Grid alerts management (MAIN)
Coordinator 1	100%	4	1,680	6,720	0.25	4.00
Number activities					8,113	149
Hours year					2,028	596

Fig. 3.1 Occupancy rates for primary tasks in Emergency Unit—Hephaestus

To lower consumption, efficiency must be improved. A lean approach is required to enhance efficiency in performing tasks. That means doing a detailed analysis of how the job is done, removing all possible wastage and reinventing actions to get rid of entrenchment. Along with that, industrialization and using technology are excellent allies in lowering consumption.

That was what Pegasus did. Its Pricing area initially estimated an LTA consumption of 20 hours in evaluation tasks. Seeing that the looming workload meant tripling the department's processors' capacity, detailed work on cutting consumption began. The following actions were undertaken to that end:

1. Handing over fact-checking to the back office
2. Classifying different groups of Pricing category by complexity
3. Automating tasks
4. Industrializing tasks

This all meant that, depending on the Pricing group concerned, final consumption dropped by between 1.17 and 5 hours.[10] This drop unlocked a lot of capacity, but not enough to meet forthcoming demand. And capacity had to be raised.

Capacity was raised by incorporating external resources. The latter took on the simplest tasks and the existing structure, with its high knowledge level focused on more complicated tasks.

Another path that perfectly complements the one just described here is the aforesaid one of spotting benchmark consumption.[11] As seen in the previous chapter, this path likewise has a very significant effect on operations culture. By seeking outstanding workers, the message is transformed into a quest for everybody's self-pride in doing a better job. This message is spectacularly

---

[10] From 20 hours to begin with, this could be considered a total success.

[11] Remember, understanding knowledge applied by the one that does the job in the least time, while sticking to the service specifications as promised.

powerful when underlining the positive and proactive approach to unlocking capacity. Along with "No hire, No fire", it pinpoints knowledge as the differential element when seeking efficiency. Remember that in its I-CAN program Achilles focused on this path and spotted the benchmarks. That enabled it to propose actions to improve knowledge stock that the rest of the team could take using TREASURE.

> Consumption is lowered by:
>
> - Acting on job efficiency.
> - Finding benchmark consumption and the knowledge that allows somebody to work that way, and transferring it to the rest of the group.

The Mix Between Primaries and Secondaries

Let us now go back to Hephaestus. After a lean analysis, Emergency decided that primary consumptions were appropriate. When analyzing secondaries, indeed it was found that considerable transformation could be undertaken to make them more efficient. The work focused on "planned work management" and "fraud management". Actions were thus designed that compressed time consumption, while applying a mobility system was analyzed for workers, in order to halve consumption. In parallel, the department's management decided to double time earmarked for fraud. The aim was to boost detection and achieve synergies with a new activity, that is, remotely metering big consumers.

The next step was to analyze whether Emergency had enough people to respond to incoming requests. A capacity matrix was used for that. A capacity matrix is a table where coordinators' occupancy rates are calculated depending on the call log. To draw up the capacity matrix, we have to know the demand load or an approximation thereof.

Emergency first did the calculation using just primary activities. In primary activities, or principal activity as they called it, the occupancy rate, depending on the shift, varied from 39% to 6%. The director found this acceptable, as his aim was to fill his coordinators' time with secondary activities. To do that, secondary activities were analyzed using the same capacity matrix. Secondary activities had an occupancy rate (depending on shifts) of 56–52%. Therefore, it could be assumed that the Emergency team should not take on more primary tasks, but it could make room for some secondaries, above all on evening/night shifts.

MORNING SHIFT	FTE	No.	UNIT CAPACITY hours/ hours	TOTAL CAPACITY	Home notification management (MAIN)	Grid notification management (MAIN)	Planned work management	Fraud management	Third-party damage management	Dispatching alerts management, CTR	Supervision emissions distribution reports	Check workers' equipment	Other improvement actions	XX	XY	AVERAGE CONSUMPTION	NEW OCCUPANCY LEVEL	CURRENT OCCUPANCY LEVEL
Coordinator1	100%	4	1,680	6,720	0.25	4.00	0.009	0.09	1.00	0.31	0.32	1.31		0.05	1.00	4,534	67%	56%
% Activity/Total					48.49%	14.25%	3.01%	12.55%	0.00%	8.37%	0.00%	2.51%	0.00%	5.80%	5.02%			
																2,624	39%	39%
																MAIN ACTIVITY		

Fig. 3.2 A coordinator's current capacity matrix at Emergency Unit—Hephaestus

Let us analyze Fig. 3.2. It shows a coordinator's current capacity matrix. Readers should note that two columns have been added, headed XX and XY. They will be for the new jobs Emergency will take on as part of their secondary tasks. The primaries will stay the same.

An issue to be analyzed is whether the percentage mix of primaries and secondaries is right for keeping the promise. (In Fig. 3.2, the line "% of total activity" considers each group's tasks as a percentage of the total.) Remember that the priorities in Hephaestus' Promise are time reliability (keeping to what is promised) and response time. Given that any LTA occupancy rate in services greater than 80% leads to backlogs, an occupancy rate of 39% for the morning shift (bottom right cell in Fig. 3.2) for Emergency's primary tasks seems reasonable. This percentage falls to 31% for the late shift and 6% for the night shift. This tells us that the late and night shifts may have a higher proportion of secondary tasks assigned to them.

Take note. The percentage mix of primary and secondary tasks is a strategic—not operational—decision and thus its owner is the MD. The MD must bear in mind that as it is an LTA, backlogs may arise even if the occupancy rate is low. And its percentage breakdown must be analyzed by weighting the priorities and the effect the mix will have on the service. Studying the log is usually an asset when taking decisions in this area.

At Hephaestus, it was decided that the mix was suitable, as were the time slots used. As the day shift had a higher occupancy rate than the late or night shift, contingency plans were drawn up in the unlikely event of a peak that could not be covered. Meaning that one shift could ask for more hands from another in case of emergency. Such considerations led to running preventive plans for increasing capacity, which specified ways to proceed in emergency mode and rectified possible contingencies.

At Hephaestus Emergency, this action was especially important given that response time for primaries was zero minutes. If we recall the Achilles example, this allows greater room for maneuver by defining as primary everything that happens before market close at 4 p.m. But gas is gas, and when there is an emergency, it must be fixed without a moment's delay!

Once the primary mix is settled, the percentage occupancy rate of the secondaries must be considered. Well, 100 minus primaries, readers will think. In other words $100 - 39 = 61\%$. Well, that depends.[12] An average is an average and has its peaks and troughs. Defining 100% capacity utilization means there will be a backlog for some issues. It is therefore essential that brainpower has clear prioritizing criteria. Because there will be occasional backlogs. Thinking otherwise is to bury one's head in the sand.

Obviously, everything much depends on the type of secondaries under analysis. There are tasks where responding at one time or another makes no difference. There are tasks that, although they may be planned for, require total reliability when delivered, and if an agent has a wide swing in incoming demand for primaries, they will see their planning tumble down like mikado sticks. For all those reasons, the mix is a strategic decision that, regrettably, events often turn into an operational one. In other words, the decision is taken by a manager that does not see the big picture needed to assess its impact.

This is a difficult issue to get across, and I would love to be able to write that all of our four companies have absorbed and made it their own. But to be sincere, I believe Hephaestus has gotten the most out of it. It is hard for the others to understand that, wish as they might, if occupancy rates are very high, then something will fall by the wayside! Unfortunately, the world is what it is, not what we would like it to be; and if this issue is not tackled, there will always be service breakdowns. Clarity and transparency are a fixed requisite, and always, always remember that in Operations somebody always has to decide. If the manager will not, somebody else will instead, and usually their criteria do not match.

Returning to Hephaestus. In work group meetings, it was found that Emergency could incorporate other secondary tasks from the Operations Department (XX and XY in Fig. 3.2). That would unlock capacity in Operations that could thus start a much sought-after service design action, to give clients better provisions.

The new tasks transferred were much in line with activities already performed by the Emergency Unit, and they concentrated on "following up video surveillance and responding to alarms" and "managing remote industrial metering". New responsibilities proceeded alongside a specific training plan that filled in existing knowledge gaps. Solving and tackling these new problems, to the degree the service promised, required coordinators to learn new terms.

---

[12] The magic word in Operations is that everything depends on something, Promise, essence, service design, and much else besides.

Artemis: Unlocking Hotel Managers' Capacity

The family owning Artemis wanted their hotel managers to spend 50% of their time on looking after the service essence and staying focused on everyday events outside the office. They are close-knit, family hotels and, as we have seen, client contact is a very important part of fulfilling their essence.

In a work group meeting with the Family, it was decided that the appropriate structure for a manager's tasks would be the one shown in Fig. 3.3: 50% out of office, 15% for personal matters, 20% for checking and follow-up and 15% for miscellaneous matters.

The real situation was quite different (Fig. 3.4), and managers spent many hours on what they called office tasks. This time, thus spent, undermined the time available for the out-of-office tasks the Family were after. Only one of the hotels (hotel 5) already followed the indications in the sought-after service strategy.

That situation put resource allocation on the agenda. Each hotel had an administrator that backed up the manager and reported to management in head office. Spending 50% on out-of-office tasks meant managers had to delegate tasks that they were then performing to the administrator. The manager-administrator operating mode was different in every hotel, and by the same token so were the tasks handed down in each hotel.

The first job to do was analyze what administrative tasks each manager was doing, how they could be industrialized and what know-how could be derived. The aim was to harmonize jobs and responsibilities while keeping each hotel's individual character. Hotel 5 was used as a baseline for understanding how the manager worked with his administrator. Likewise, in hotel 6 the manager did

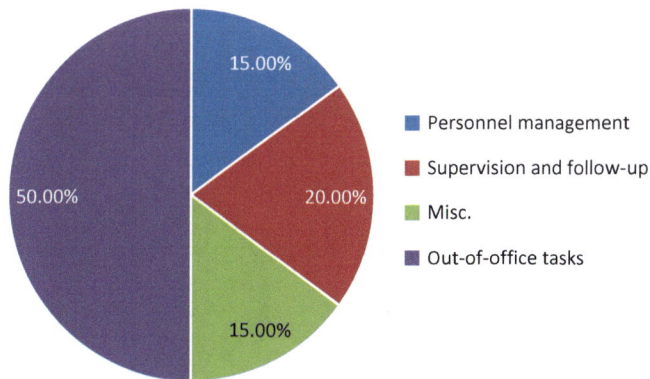

Fig. 3.3 Appropriate time structure for a hotel manager at Artemis

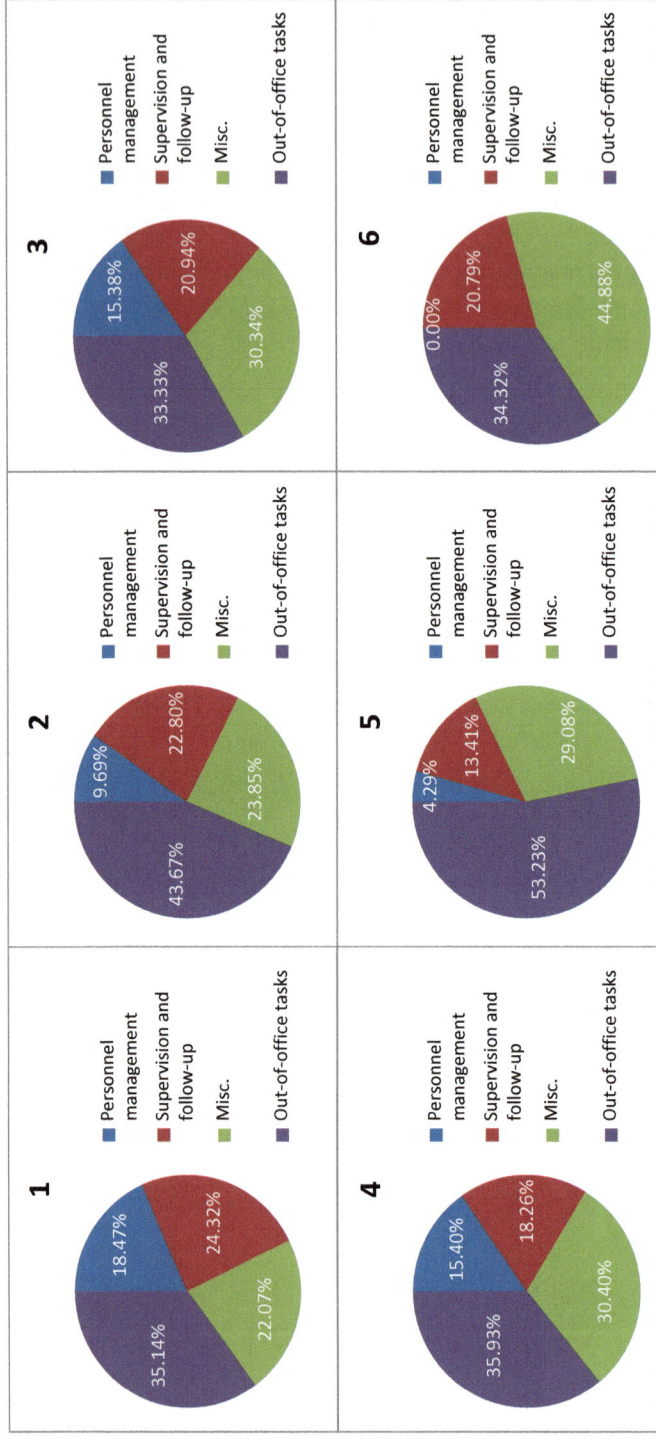

Fig. 3.4 Actual time structure for the hotels managers at Artemis

not manage staff, because such functions were delegated entirely to the administrator. This fact was also used as a case study to understand how they were organized.[13]

As a first step toward unlocking capacity, each hotel manager briefed the Operations manager on the tasks they performed (see Table 3.1) and which ones they figured they could delegate to the administrators.

In parallel, the administration manager performed an initial capacity analysis of the administrators' current situation. Figure 3.5 shows the load matrix

Table 3.1 Artemis hotel manager's job description

I. Staff management	Email replies to client requests, complaints or orders (reception helps)
Contract or call up and check contract termination	
	Check groups, conference rooms, visits and other commercial orders
Check overtime and public holidays	Budgets and investment plan
Check days off sick, medical reports and request physicals	Plan off-season work
Check staff by occupation	Follow up hotel online pricing and occupancy
Practical staff management	Corporate orders
Report month-end variables	
Payroll delivery	**III. Miscellaneous**
Follow up department heads, check and fill staff crunches	Receive outside visits: suppliers, creditors, contractors, etc.
Check days off and vacations	Follow up tripadvisor/booking/holidaycheck sites
Plan physicals	
Plan and organize training courses	Receive department heads, problem-solving and operations
Meet with the works council	Receive staff in office
Attend work inspections	Receive clients in office
	Take outside calls
II. Check and follow-up	Brief with assistant manager
Weekly operations report (Fridays)	Receive, read and analyze in-house questionnaires
Check and follow up projections, bottom line and earnings report	
Monthly report	Manage email
Follow up and send minutes of quality and department head meetings	Miscellaneous management: suppliers, creditors, general services, etc.
Follow up and check hygiene-health indicators	Daily analysis bookings/occupancy and action on reception/commercial
Follow up, check and sign invoices	Court cases
Check and sign vouchers, invitations, cancellations and house account	Hotel posters (in-house shows, menus, allergy warnings, etc.)
Administration tasks, municipal or regional fines or sanctions (e.g. commercial premises)	Check VP channel (and design posters)
Follow up and response quality reports for owners and management	Meet with hotel administrator
Check entertainment program, changes, requests or improvements depending on occupation and feasibility	

---

[13] Hotel 6 is the biggest hotel in Spain.

PROCESSORS	Number	mins month	TOTAL min/month	Accounts	Reports	Personnel	Misc.	AVG. CONSUMPTION	OCCUPANCY
Admin. Hotel 1	1.40	10,560	14,784	11	113	1	24	12,628	85%
Admin. Hotel 2	0.80	10,560	8,448	11	108	2	48	7,542	89%
Admin. Hotel 3	0.88	10,560	9,240	11	118	1	24	7,970	86%
Admin. Hotel 4	1.00	10,560	10,560	10	215	13	18	9,194	87%
Admin. Hotel 5	1.00	10,560	10,560	10	123	13	18	7,604	72%
Admin. Hotel 6	2.88	10,560	30,360	13	113	57	35	24,704	81%

Fig. 3.5 Load matrix of administrators

Admin. Hotel 1	1070
Admin. Hotel 2	612
Admin. Hotel 3	684.48
Admin. Hotel 4	672.4
Admin. Hotel 5	612
Admin. Hotel 6	1070

Fig. 3.6 Demand for administrative tasks

and Fig. 3.6 the average demand of administrative tasks on each hotel's administrator.

What percentage of this load could be planned for was analyzed, and it was estimated that more than 90% could be, as the percentage was low for tasks needing to be done in zero minutes. The occupancy rate of nearly 85% seemed, therefore, appropriate.[14]

It was observed that the administrator of hotel 5 had a lower occupancy rate than the others and was only a processor. That same hotel's manager was out of the office more than 50% of the time. That meant the manager did almost no administrative tasks, and furthermore, his administrator had the lowest occupancy rate in the group! They had to urgently look into what was going on in that hotel. A detailed analysis of the causes found that the administrator of hotel 5 had been with the company a long time, had mastered his job and did it with less time consumed than his colleagues in other hotels. He was the benchmark to be learned from.

Hotel 6 was then analyzed in parallel. As the hotel with most beds in Spain, the manager had a powerful Administration department that had devised all sorts of spreadsheets, Excel files and software to help with its tasks. They had

---

[14] If tasks can be planned for and there is not much randomization, occupancy may be raised without causing backlogs. It is uncertainty that causes randomization and that makes backlogs mushroom. But do not forget: "If it is not there, it is not there." If the occupancy rate is close to 85–90%, the odds of backlogs arising are very high.

PROCESSORS	Number	mins month	TOTAL min/month	Accounts	Reports	Personnel	Misc.	AVG. CONSUMPTION	OCCUPANCY
Admin. Hotel 1	1.40	10,560	14,784	11	113	13	24	14,790	100%
Admin. Hotel 2	0.80	10,560	8,448	11	108	13	48	8,684	103%
Admin. Hotel 3	0.88	10,560	9,240	11	118	13	24	9,337	101%
Admin. Hotel 4	1.00	10,560	10,560	10	215	13	18	9,194	87%
Admin. Hotel 5	1.00	10,560	10,560	10	123	13	18	7,604	72%
Admin. Hotel 6	2.88	10,560	30,360	13	113	57	35	24,704	81%

Fig. 3.7 Occupancy adding administrative duties previously performed by managers

industrialized and the rest had to copy those improvements. The whole of Artemis learned from those two hotels.

After spotting the tasks that needed to be delegated to the administrators,[15] a load analysis was performed again. It was seen that occupancy rates exceeded 100% in some situations (Fig. 3.7). In others, as in hotels 4, 5 and 6, occupancy stayed the same, as the administrator had previously freed the manager from all administrative duties.

In hotels 1, 2 and 3, if administrators were to take on the managers' load, then administrators' capacity needed to be unlocked.[16] To do that, all the administrators were asked to pool all the individual improvements they had made in recent years. Thus, a catalog was compiled of actions undertaken in the various hotels to compress consumption and industrialize.

Meetings were held with the two benchmark hotels to spot/transfer knowledge with the rest and lean simplification actions were taken to enhance the use of time. For example, as the group of smaller-sized hotels was all located a reasonable distance from each other, one of the administrators was detailed to collect each one's takings and take them to the bank, instead of each administrator personally doing so. Likewise, daily visits to head office were done away with and replaced with paperless activity. All these moves unlocked capacity (Fig. 3.8), but were not enough to reach the occupancy rate that the service level required. Therefore, some administrators' involvement needed to be raised (Fig. 3.9). The target average occupancy rate was 80–85%. To that end, hotels 1, 2 and 3 raised their capacity by an average of another 14–25%.

This work was very fulfilling for every participant. They understood how individual improvement actions could not be relegated solely to the hotel where they occurred, but had to be spread around to achieve progress. The domino effect of unlocking capacity showed how harmonizing occupations unlocked capacity to undertake greater value-added tasks. A fact is worth more than a thousand words. Thus, I always advocate running pilot schemes

---

[15] To unlock the managers' capacity.

[16] Readers will understand perfectly that this is a domino effect, which often ends up with technology doing jobs that nobody wants to do, or that it does better than humans.

PROCESSORS	Number	mins month	TOTAL min/month	Accounts	Reports	Personnel	Misc.	AVG. CONSUMPTION	OCCUPANCY
Adm Hotel 1	1.60	10,560	16,896	11	113	13	24	14,790	88%
Adm Hotel 2	1.00	10,560	10,560	11	108	13	48	8,684	82%
Adm Hotel 3	1.00	10,560	10,560	11	118	13	24	9,337	88%
Adm Hotel 4	1.00	10,560	10,560	10	215	13	18	9,194	87%
Adm Hotel 5	1.00	10,560	10,560	10	123	13	18	7,604	72%
Adm Hotel 6	2.88	10,560	30,360	13	113	57	35	24,704	81%

Fig. 3.8 Occupancy rate after unlocked capacity

PROCESSORS	Number	Number
Admin. Hotel 1	1.40	1.60
Admin. Hotel 2	0.80	1.00
Admin. Hotel 3	0.88	1.00
Admin. Hotel 4	1.00	1.00
Admin. Hotel 5	1.00	1.00
Admin. Hotel 6	2.88	2.88

Fig. 3.9 Capacity increase required

that show the benefits of applying ideas. Capacity analysis is so absolutely overwhelming at proving empirically that to do so in only one area triggers a very important domino effect.

Every company I have worked with realizes the importance of performing capacity analyses to understand how to unlock capacity. For example, Hephaestus defined the importance of capacity analyses thus: "It is the essential way to squeeze out available resources to structure ourselves effectively and give internal and external clients a five-star service." And they specified that in eight points, which I believe provide food for thought when applying capacity analyses to any company:

1. Know what we are facing in every job function, analyze the current situation and spot shortfalls and breakdowns to redirect them as innovations.
2. Achieving *sustainable efficiency* in Hephaestus. Remember that cost-cutting does not lead to efficiency, but efficiency does lead to cutting costs.
3. Spotting activities that can be industrialized and substituted by others of greater value.
4. Negotiate with our managers using facts and not opinions.
5. Have a staff that agrees with our company's needs.
6. Benefit as much as possible from the resources we have currently available.
7. Make our operating dreams come true.
8. Achieve excellence in our service and be the best.

At Hephaestus, when performing a capacity analysis[17] each department head was asked how they could be more efficient and what was their operations dream. These questions drew out ideas for improvement that had always been inside brainpower's heads, and enabled concrete action plans for unlocking capacity. This action by Hephaestus echoes what was written above about Achilles's I-CAN, and proves that when room for thought is provided, and methodologically channeled, brainpower accepts the challenge and makes proposals. And very reasonable proposals, too. Both measures sold pro-actively the value of capacity analyses and both have gotten the brains and their companies very good results. But we should never forget the importance of keeping up the work. As a member of Achilles's G12 said: "The risk we are seeing is that if we don't keep up the I-CAN results, it all comes to nothing."

We need to insist constantly. I-CAN had to introduce a final checklist so the area manager could gather abbreviated results of efficiency and unlocked capacity, and follow up on the measures. As we shall see, Pegasus also did so in another format. Perseverance and following-up are two constants in making things happen.

Unlocking Capacity to Handle Servitization[18]

As an endnote to the experiences detailed in this chapter, I shall cite what a Portuguese company is going through, one that works in Africa and wishes to change from selling products to selling services. This is so-called servitization.

To ponder the changes to be made, the CEO organized a couple of days' internal brainstorming. And he figured, SPDM could provide a good methodological framework to help his group of 50 managers think things over. The owners as well as the board of directors took part, as well as the top tier in the group's various companies and extended enterprise.

The SPDM analysis revealed an interesting situation. The company owners wanted transformation, and the managers understood that. But there was a snag. Switching to selling services from selling products immediately requires action: unlocking capacity in the whole internal as well as extended management team. They had to keep doing what they were doing and, moreover,

---

[17] We should remember that at Hephaestus capacity analysis was the responsibility of HR department. This introduced an aspect of improvement that added much value.

[18] Term coined by Andy Neely, of the University of Cambridge, UK: "Servitization is a transformation journey—it involves firms (often manufacturing firms) developing the capabilities they need to provide services and solutions that supplement their traditional product offerings."

learn how to do new things, and there are only 24 hours in a day.[19] Management believed firmly in "No hire, No fire." There was no need to take on people; they wanted to transform how they did things by changing the narrative and changing the way they proceeded. Selling electric turbines is one thing, selling services is quite another. They needed to redesign the value proposition and service. And that takes time. Time to rearrange, to change vocabulary and to study new problems that will arise.

For example, an interesting problem. Their interlocutors-clients change every two to three years. It is the way things are done in those countries, given that their clients are mainly local administrators. Selling a product is something very defined, perfectly specified, concrete and one-shot. A service is more abstract, with many more individual readings. The question the managers were asking was: "How do I keep the service sustainable if each interlocutor comes along with a different expectations portfolio?" To this question is added how to define the service's value proposition, following up the service specification and knowledge needed to express and following up said service. The change is drastic. We are not talking about unlocking capacity, but rethinking the whole SPDM model.

I reckon that understanding this case's implications is crucial. Beginning a capacity analysis may be a task that leads to concrete results. That is the case with Hephaestus or Artemis. It may also be a concrete task that leads to rethinking partially the knowledge needed and delving into pondering reorganization, extended enterprise and using technology. Take Pegasus in its Pricing area or the I-CAN/TREASURE combination at Achilles. Or it may open a Pandora's box, as it did in this Portuguese company. The crucial thing is to spot the impact the action entails.

Unlocking capacity for servitization in this Portuguese company meant going down the road to rearranging the whole operations strategy. The turbines will still be sold, and everything done thus far to get there works. But the packaging will be different and provisions that accompany it, too. The unlocked capacity will serve to buy time to redesign the service conceptually, spot needs that new provisions entail, and enhance the knowledge stock that will allow new problems to be faced. It is a joint job for the whole management team and the extended enterprise. They must all redesign the service to act five minutes ahead of the blockages that will arise.

---

[19] Although as an African manager in the group told me, the concept of time is totally different in the two continents. Effectively, cultural aspects must be taken into account and may well change task consumption, but the basic ideas work across cultures.

How can that be done? The next chapter tackles how to face this situation using service design. Building on classic ideas, clients are no longer demographic, but ethnographic and grouped into tribes. Designing a service requires redefining the operations settings and that starts with understanding that the contribution margin is the best indicator of operational efficiency.

SPDM Concepts Used in This Chapter

Chapters referred to: 4 and 5

The most relevant concepts used in this chapter are capacity analysis, lean action and time structuring.

A capacity analysis starts with the premise that in one hour there is one hour's time. And therefore, if we find out how much time a task consumes, we may know how many tasks we can produce in an hour. Put simply, if 5 minutes are consumed on a task, we can produce 12 minutes per hour, that is, the result of dividing 60/5. And if we are in a service where 24 people turn up per hour as a long-term average (LTA), then we have two options. Either halve consumption and make it two minutes and a half, or hire another person. The obvious way to go is compress the task time.

That can be done using lean techniques. In SPDM, this is done by analyzing the six operations variables: processes, times, operations rules, information system, knowledge stock and capacity.

Time deserves a special mention. The seven times offer a time structuring that allows hidden inefficiencies to be tackled when handling this crucial component. The operations time, which is the commonly known time, is usually just 30% of total time. The remaining 70% are times that must be tackled in order to eliminate them (point I in the Conceptual Appendix).

Once time is compressed, it must be found whether tasks performed are primary or secondary (point II in the Conceptual Appendix). Primary tasks are those that require zero minutes response time. Secondary tasks are those that may be planned for and executed whenever it suits the processor.

The next step is to draw up a capacity matrix (point III in the Conceptual Appendix). The capacity matrix makes for analyzing the service output that can be done, and spots the bottleneck, the processor that produces least. Capacity analysis is the first step toward understanding the service's efficiency. For that, a matrix may be charted at first by using primaries to understand the stress the service suffers when zero-minute response time activities are performed.

The mix concept is introduced in that matrix. The mix is the percentage of different components of the services portfolio. If, for example, a service portfolio consists of five service groupings, each grouping has a percentage of the total service. It is interesting to distinguish between strategic mix—what we want to happen—and the real mix—what really happens. The bottleneck varies according to the mix's breakdown. The CEO defines the mix and it reflects company strategy.

The load matrix (point IV in the Conceptual Appendix) spots the processors' occupancy rate for a given demand. If the mix in a capacity matrix is expressed in percentages, in the load matrix it is done with whole numbers. The end result is that processors' LTA occupancy rates are found. In services, an LTA occupancy rate greater than 80% means delays and backlogs.

The load matrix is absolutely essential in the quest for unlocking capacity. It finds the servers' average occupancy rate. Done individually, it can spot benchmark occupancy levels and help to find those processors that are doing tasks much more efficiently, and can show the rest how it is done.

Chapter 3: Conceptual Appendix

I. The seven times

Time type	Questions
1. Operation: standard time to perform tasks	Can we compress activity time?
	Can we increase processor productivity?
	Can we better combine technology with the activity?
2. Preparation: standard time to perform tasks	Can we eliminate changes?
	Can we eliminate preparation?
	Can we prepare out of clients' sight?
	Can we improve ways to change the task?
3. Batch: waiting time to travel together	Can we cut batch size?
	Can we eliminate economies of scale due to the batch?
	Can we smooth flow so that it is done by unit?
4. Interference: waiting time, random	Can we make appointments?
	Can we cut service variability?
	Can we make waiting profitable?
	Can we diversify capacity?
5. Planning: time due to planning	Can we eliminate variability in arrivals?
	Can we change capacity easily?
6. Safety: time just in case	Can we cut delays?
	And variability during them?
	Can we penalize latecomers?
7. Disruption: forgetfulness time	Are there inexplicable delays?
	Explain the inexplicable

II. Primary and secondary tasks

Processor	
Primary Tasks	Secondary Tasks
Total hours/week	Total hours/week

III. Capacity matrix

Processors	nº	Hours/month	Total capacity	Service 1	Service 2	Service 3	Service 4	Service 5	Average consumption	Output
Station 1										
Station 2										
Station 3										
Station 4										
Station 5										

MIX %

- Processors: types of job function (list them).
- Number of positions in each job function (number of processors).
- Number of hours worked per year per worker: normally, contract hours are used, but if company has more advantageous conditions over the application agreement, adjust said quantities.
- Number of total hours available = number of processors x number of hours worked per year.

IV. Load Matrix

Processors	nº	Hours/month	Total capacity	Service 1	Service 2	Service 3	Service 4	Service 5	Average consumption	Utilization rate
Station 1										
Station 2										
Station 3										
Station 4										
Station 5										

MIX Nº

- The difference between a capacity and the load matrix is that in the latter we already have a target number of clients (a determined load) and using this number we convert the mix into whole numbers (by multiplying the load by the % of each component in the mix).
- The occupancy given in the end column is each processor's real occupancy rate.

4

The Contribution Margin and Tribes

Abstract A client should no longer be viewed demographically but anthropologically, according to their behavior. Operations efficiency is assessed using the contribution margin, and a key aspect of it is spotting the client's ethnographic needs and their customer journey. By using the SPDM version of the customer journey, two companies show how they used this tool and how such methodology provided a concrete plan to enhance their service.

The main thrust of this chapter is to introduce service design as a powerful tool for boosting profitability and sustainability. We start out with the basic hypothesis that we do not do "No".[1] Accepting that hypothesis means looking at problems from a different standpoint. From another angle, in another ecosystem. As we say colloquially, to turn things on their head. Using this new standpoint, blocking factors that seemed impossible to get rid of now tumble down like sand castles. Different premises are used when analyzing, and you only get optimal solutions when seen from a service design perspective.

Intertwined with this argument is accepting that the contribution margin is a very efficient guide to assessing pro-actively[2] whether the service design is operationally on target. Service design stems from the Promise and deviations from, or swings in, the margin provide information about the actual way operations are translated. Following the margin and watching its tendencies is

---

[1] Please, get rid of this cuss word. Everything is possible; you just have to keep trying from a different perspective. Nothing comes for free, but everything can be achieved if one understands, learns, tries and perseveres.

[2] Never reactively. Always ahead of the problem, prevention is essential!

© The Author(s) 2019
B. Muñoz-Seca, *How to Get Things Right*, IESE Business Collection,
https://doi.org/10.1007/978-3-030-14088-5_4

a wonderful tool for detecting future problems by acting five minutes ahead.[3] Nothing stands still and constant change requires constant supervision to spot present erosion or future trends. Margin erosion is a symptom of illness. And the illness is inappropriate service design.

Deviations should prompt querying whether some change has caused modifications that require redesigning the service. Such redesigning may consist of deft brush strokes, or major surgery may be needed. Whatever the case, it will require changes in the operational settings.

Let us analyze the specific case of the Pena Palace[4] in the National Park of the same name near Sintra (Machado, 2018), in Portugal. In a seminar on service excellence, one of the most nagging problems they had was analyzed: waiting times in the line to enter the site.

To start with, the production problem with ticket sales was analyzed. Next, the need to hire more ticket sellers was mooted, to reduce waiting times.

Following the "No hire, No fire" mantra, actions began to be proposed to provide ways other than buying tickets to minimize the physical inflow at the ticket booths. Processing was streamlined using a lean approach to improving operations. But the core problem persisted. Peak demand for the service at the entrance, as well as by palace visitors, were incompatible with the sought-after Promise. The alternative that arose was to do like the Alhambra in Granada, Spain, where they had introduced an operational strategy of restricted ticket sales.

We stopped the discussion there and proceeded to find out who the clients were that went to the Palace. The clients' anthropological—not the demographic—profile was sought. These are the so-called tribes, groups with similar sociological backgrounds.[5] A detailed analysis of these groups led us to an obvious move: the service had to be redesigned. Distinguishing between service given to different tribes opened up possibilities that had not been considered before. Some examples: there were tribes whose special cultural interest led to offering visits with a more complete portfolio of cultural services, outside normal Palace opening hours, and that allowed a much higher fee to be charged[6] than the one for normal hours. Other tribes did not want a standard visit: their overwhelming desire was to take photos of themselves at the Palace's

---

[3] Statistical process control (SPC) is another wonderful preventive tool. SPC detects deviations from a machine's average function and warns of possible problems. Plotting the contribution margin graph may be used for exactly the same end.

[4] The Pena National Palace was one of the Portuguese royal family's main residences in the nineteenth century and is also one of the ultimate expressions of nineteenth-century romanticism in Portugal.

[5] Anthropologists have always studied such behavior and ethnography has been their main tool.

[6] This is already in place in other sites such as the Inca city of Machu Picchu, in Peru. If visitors do not wish to enter with mainstream tourists, they can arrange an after-hours visit. A specialized guide will walk them through the ruins and explain them in detail. Neither the price nor the experience is the same.

highlights, so their tour could be reduced to half a standard one, and follow a totally different visitor flow.

Result? A different service proposition concept based on clients' anthropological needs.[7] Distinguishing between needs and providing a services portfolio that can break down demand and streamline operational efficiency to improve service. That is what is needed. Neither spotting the tribes nor designing a service in keeping with their needs eats into the margin. The "obvious" solution for the Palace was to increase the number of ticket sellers. The optimal solution is redesigning the service. It keeps the promise and does not erode the margin.

The Customer Journey and Service Problems

Hephaestus wanted to understand their end customer better to become a more customer-centric company. To do that, they needed to understand the customer journey, spot existing tribes of clients, who served them (Hephaestus or the extended enterprise) and design a service portfolio accordingly. A Hephaestus work group focused on those tasks.

Hephaestus's star activity for client contact was periodic inspections (PIs). Client no-shows or lack of punctuality were causing service breakdowns that sparked tension among clients as well as in the extended enterprise. Figure 4.1 shows the % success rate for visits in performing PIs by time slot in 2017. Time slots should provide 100% of the service as planned and executed. Percentages show the real percentage compliance. Those figures led to inefficiency[8] in the extended enterprise and dissatisfied end customers.

As a first step, the work group gathered data of the actual situation. To do that, the following measures were taken over a three-week period:

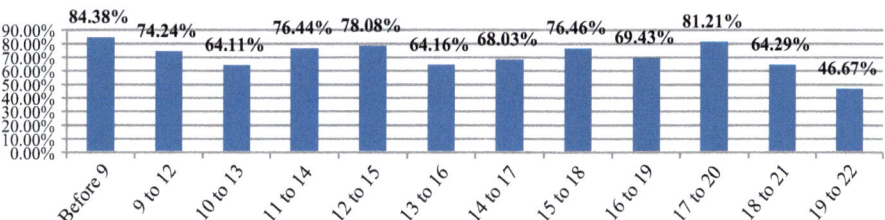

Fig. 4.1 % Success

---

[7] Madrid's Prado Museum has just introduced plans with different lengths of visiting time for different client groups. Ranging from one hour for 15 pictures, to three hours. À la carte service.

[8] Having to reschedule visits, contact the client and so on. It is all reprocessing.

- Questions were thrown at the call center (CC) about service provision, a meeting was held with the CC supervisor and the CC was visited physically.
- Meetings were held with the extended enterprise to spot customer types and problems found.
- Complaints and claims were reviewed.
- Meetings were held about PI issues with other Hephaestus departments that interacted with clients.

All this information was condensed, categorized and written down on different-colored bits of paper according to the category of problem (Fig. 4.2). Following were the predefined categories:

1. General customer service problems
2. Service provision problems
3. Blocking factors preventing action
4. Customer types

Once classified by categories, they were placed in the Operations director's office for all of Hephaestus to read, and contribute nuances or new ideas if necessary. The wall became a center for attention about the work in progress.

Next, in a case study session, the customer service group split categories up into four groups using KJ[9] methodology. The outcome of this work was to classify problems detected as follows:

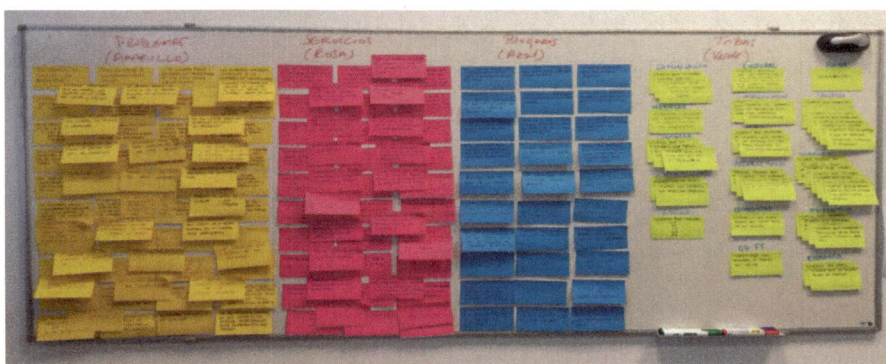

Fig. 4.2 Problems classified by color/category

---

[9]KJ Method: approach devised by Shoji Shiba, which starts off by listing concepts that have a common affinity with pictures.

- Problems caused by the tribes' features
- Hephaestus's problems in general due to its idiosyncratic service
- Improvements that must be implemented at Hephaestus
- Blockages caused by:
  - Clients imposing their own standards
  - Rulebook
  - Extended enterprise
  - Hephaestus's internal problems

As a first step in tackling actions for the improvement that this list of problems called for, the Hephaestus group decided that it must begin by understanding the profile of the tribes on the service's receiving end. Concern over providing good service along with a contribution margin made approaching the job this way indispensable.

Hephaestus's Tribes

Drawing from the list of problems those features that defined customer types, the work group, after a KJ exercise, defined 11 groups based on anthropological and sociological similarity among customer profiles. We called those 11 groups "tribes", in keeping with their anthropological content:

1. Sybarites
2. Comfortable
3. Limited economic means
4. Want direct contact
5. Different cultures + languages
6. Aggressive
7. Techies
8. Seniors
9. Mental grandparents
10. Affected
11. Rebels

Definition of each Customer Archetype at Hephaestus

1. *Sybarites*: Require special, personalized and refined treatment, will stand no nonsense. Require their distributor at their service and consider themselves unique customers.
2. *Comfortable*: Ask the companies for a quiet life with no fuss or headaches, as any problem will hurt their pockets.
3. *Limited economic means*: Purchasing power has been hit by working and/or family conditions, cannot bear the cost of measures they do not see as priorities.
4. *Want direct contact.* Want direct contact with Hephaestus, trusting it will solve every request/problem processed and think this is the most effective way.
5. *Different cultures + languages.* Due to their place of birth/residence they are used to things being done differently in the same situations arising in Spain, where the language has influence as a communications channel.
6. *Aggressive.* Temperamental. The only way they can get what they want is by laying down the law and, if they do not get it, they cause physical and/or verbal conflicts and disdain any attempt to help.
7. *Techies.* New technologies are used to communicate and manage, and they will use no other means if they are not up to the same standard.
8. *Seniors.* Communication and management are done by traditional means. Wary of change, little capacity to adapt. Need proof before accepting change.
9. *Mental grandparents.* Limited in action and/or dependent. Incapable of managing any obligation by themselves.
10. Smug attitude: They think they know everything and are in continual possession of the truth. Always seek contact with the superior, as nobody else will do when handling their request.
11. *Rebels*: Always at odds with any action taken, cause more problems than those which may actually arise and make the journey longer and more tiresome.

As a second step, Hephaestus stressed cross-referencing each tribe with certain customer features that had been found in the initial investigative work. The features were listed and classified into three groups by (descending) importance: A ++, B + y C – (Table 4.1).

A matrix was drawn up to cross-reference each archetype with each feature, by spotting what features were important for each archetype. For example, one of Hephaestus's areas found that its industrial as well as commercial customers were of the "comfortable" archetype and not very tech-savvy. This was a tipping point for ruling out new tech-centered service provisions.

This exercise not only clarified finding each tribe's composition but also showed that 11 archetypes were too many to deftly undertake service actions. The customer area thus decided to draw up a group of archetypes to provide

Table 4.1 Independent features of each archetype

A	B	C
Unaware of Hephaestus's existence	Consumes little	A stickler for the rules
Commercial, industrial or domestic customer	Cares not for the rules	Fearful
Has limited time		Feel they are VIPs
Big consumer		

a first draft of service actions. The grouping exercise drew up the following four clusters:

- **Cluster 1.**
  - Sybarites
  - Comfortable
  - Limited economic means

- **Cluster 2.**
  - Want direct contact
  - Different cultures + languages
  - Aggressive

- **Cluster 3.**
  - Techies
  - Seniors

- **Cluster 4.**
  - Mental grandparents
  - Affected
  - Rebels

The group again cross-referenced clusters with A features in order to begin designing a service adapted to the needs of archetype clusters.

Then they went back to the initial list of problems and designed actions for improvement that responded to problems found in PIs. This list of actions very much bore in mind that the extended enterprise provided the service, and that meant working closely with it (Table 4.2).

The action plan was shared with the management team and the MD allocated resources to implement it. The archetypes defined the new customer profile and provided the basis for the next stage: the customer journey.

Table 4.2 Some blockages in Hephaestus's PI service

Blockages			
Cause of blockage	Types of blockage	Action plan	In charge
Blockages in the extended enterprise	Worker indifferent to customer satisfaction, is not bothered	Meeting to explain customers' importance, launch campaign, brief on process, rules of the game, etc.	Management/PI Dept.
		Work group as extended enterprise	PI Dept. with help from management
		Analyze customer complaints and sanctions in case of proven repetition	PI Dept.
		Training employees how Hephaestus wants customers treated (extended enterprise training)	PI Dept. with help from management
		Extranet with extended enterprise (continuous communication)	PI Dept.
		Employee of the month ranking, with gift	PI Dept.
		Improvement and support for analyzing planning, correcting deviations on time, and demanding greater effectiveness in fulfilling plans	PI Dept.

The Customer Journey and KPIs[10]

Hephaestus wanted to design a new PI service. The "customer journey" method provided a basis for spotting a new way to provide it. The journey spots the service's most important touchpoints (TPs) today. Then it splits up the service into five stages, how customers find a TP, how they join the service, how they use it, how they extend new services stemming from that TP and how they quit the TP (Fig. 4.3). To quit the TP is not to quit the service; it is quitting that particular touchpoint. For example, calling the call center to arrange an appointment.

The journey considers the service here and now spots customer needs, prompts dreaming about provisions the service must provide and highlights blocking factors that surface. This exercise can be very positive for spurring creativity in any group that wishes to reset a service. It is very much a keep it simple and stupid (KISS) approach and unveils exploratory creativity[11] among group members.

Hephaestus spotted seven touchpoints in the PI customer journey:

1. Letters
2. Poster in home building
3. Employee
4. Calling card

---

[10] KPI: Key performance indicator, one that measures reliability in executing a parameter.
[11] There are three types of creativity; combinatory, exploratory and transformation.

TP letters	Know	Involve	Use	Extend	Quit
Description Today	Receiving letter	Reading letter	Choosing who does the PI		
Client Needs	Receive more information (what, how, PI's value)	Understanding the information provided	Choosing Hephaestus to do the PI	Requesting reminder for appointment	
Service Dream	Simple information and unique idiom (i-guide), QR code and information about the online appointments platform	Exact advance appointment	Appointment reminder by favorite channel	Financing, payment facilities, discounts and non-regulatory PI (when desired)	
Blocking Factors	Give three months notice	Does not receive letter, loses it, forgets	Has no PI and unaware it is compulsory, or has another company do PI		Takes no notice of our information and/or has another company do PI

Fig. 4.3 Customer journey

5. Extended client call
6. *Call center*
7. PI quality control log

In multiple work sessions, the group examined each TP, one by one, and went along the four journeys (description today, customer needs, service dream and blocking factors). Figure 4.3 describes the complete journey for the "letters" TP.

After customer journeys were done, the group set about redesigning their service. It defined its focus as providing a customer-centric service. A crucial element in redesigning was industrializing the customer interface. Although it had been found that some clients rejected technology, a high percentage accepted it as a communications channel, thus allowing 50% of notices to be automated. Other actions were taken, like creating and implementing new channels such as FAQs and wikis.

Redesigning the service involved the whole journey, which had to include working with the extended enterprise. The call center was revamped substantially when service levels were redesigned to offer a more proactive solution to problems with making customer appointments. The aim of the joint work was to design a reactive and proactive platform. Meanwhile, meetings were held with all the Hephaestus business units to spot mistakes and problems at the call center and to find preventive solutions for them all. The aim was to cut back drastically on complaints.

Likewise, meetings were held with the extended enterprises that physically performed the PIs. The latter provided the link in the chain needed to be able to design the service from start to finish. Hephaestus became the customer satisfaction watchdog and all other actors followed the script Hephaestus suggested. This script was guided by the Promise[12] while preserving the essence defined as "staying close".

A new design for the service settings requires new KPIs. The group homed in on the KPI for service excellence as "the percentage of no-shows in visits", "average time for repeated requests" or "volume of requests waiting to be processed". The extended enterprise's Service Level Agreements (SLAs) were also focused on end customer satisfaction. Thus, SLAs were put in place for obtaining client data (cellphone, email), "average time for assigning service" or "percentage no-shows".

Allow me to dally briefly over one of my favorite topics, SLAs.[13] If you have read me before, I shall not repeat myself. But a bit of rationality, please. The number of SLAs is directly proportional to mistrust. A participant said in class that in his company, of Nordic origin, a study had shown how inefficient SLAs were, and how efficient trust was. Personally I have no data, but experience tells me that is very true. Obviously, Hephaestus must have SLAs with its extended enterprise. Nobody denies that. But few and very specific ones. SLAs and KPIs are two sides of the same coin. Both must measure elements that help keep the Promise.

The job of making an area customer-centric likewise included action to get rid of blockages found on "journeys", by prioritizing quick wins to show progress and improvements as they went. "Zero complaints" was the area mantra. Its work continues to this day.

The Customer Journey at Artemis

An interesting way to use touchpoints is to link them to essence in order to ensure they are sustainable. They did so at Artemis. Unlocking capacity,[14] so that hotel managers could concentrate more on looking after the essence, forced the Family to spot critical TPs when translating the essence.

Two Family members took the customer journey and spotted the TPs they deemed essential for conveying *the Artemis Family invites you*. The notion of

---

[12] Promise: No more suffering in any of the extended enterprise. Flame red: Anything that adds to the client experience.

[13] Introduced as a concept in Chap. 1.

[14] See Chap. 3.

intimacy conveys that all the little details looked after at home were likewise looked after in the hotels.

The matriarch paid special attention to using flowers and plants to convey the personal touch and trust. She went personally from hotel to hotel her whole life, deciding as she went what flowers to display and how important gardens were. Such care, which had been reinforced so personally, had to be materialized so they could keep it up, even though the "family boss" no longer went to the hotels. It was up to the next generation to materialize that essence, not merely so as not to lose it, but to extend and improve it.

Immediately, it was decided that several TPs had to be sensory. Sight, touch, smell and hearing were very important elements in the customer journey at Artemis. The hotel manager had to be just as sensitive as the owners and devote his time to the whole organization, while conveying how important senses were for clients during their stay.

Being out of the office thus meant doting on critical TPs for the Family. Services are always preventive, not reactive. An environment where owners wished to provide a sensory experience must be analyzed carefully to prevent unwanted situations. Flowers cannot be seen to wilt and must be changed preventively so they are never seen to wither. But that is not just the manager's job, whose work is to mind the essence. Every hotel member must mind it.

A corridor smelling of bleach is not what is wanted. Ensuring that does not happen can only be done if the service components are clearly stated, and analytic elements conveyed, which enable following up whether reality matches expectations. Common sense does not exist, and every hotel member must be perfectly alert and aware of how important transmitting the essence is. The way to do that is by introducing TPs that function as anchors and help monitor the actual service constantly.

Table 4.3 lists the TPs found to be most important on the customer journey, for any archetype, at Artemis. These TPs must stick in the whole organization's minds. Essence linked to TPs was introduced therefore into induction courses, at the start of the season when hotels open so that workers might be keenly aware of them.

An element that sparked much discussion was the introduction of indicators to follow up how each TP measured up in reality.[15] There had to be a yardstick that was the same for everybody, and similar guidelines for action and behavior. These discussions could, at times, reach absurd limits and had

---

[15] It was work that required great patience and perseverance. Each manager had their idea, and what was wanted was to materialize the Family's wishes and blend them with the managers' experience and the financial director's OK, as many measures catapulted costs and had to be readjusted.

Table 4.3 TPs spotted by Artemis Family

I. Reception	II. Floors	III. Dining room	IV. Bar
Outside entrance	Key	Dining room entrance	Five senses
Inside entrance	Elevator ride	Five senses in dining	-Look of premises
Physical reception: Five	Entering room: smell	room	-Music
senses	Overall view: Five	Smell	-Light
Checkout	senses	Music	Clean tables
Billing	Bathroom	Contact with maître d'	Tidy table and chairs
Exiting hotel	*Amenities*	First sight buffet	Glassware and additions
	Toilet	Matching colors	How the waiter
	Shower pressure	Replacing and tidiness	approaches with tray
	Mattress	Feel of tablecloths, glass,	Contact with waiter
	Pillows	tableware, linen	Bar decor
	Feel of the sheets	Uniforms	Interaction with waiter
	Chair on balcony	Staff interaction	
	Noise	Cook interface	
	Heating/air conditioning		
V. Entertainment	**VI. Communal areas**		
Entertainment schedule on	Garden journey		
screens	Lighting in gardens		
Interface with entertainer	Pools		
Client introduction to	Terrace journey		
entertainment staff			
Performing activity			

to be steered pro-actively. But they were likewise enriching, as they went into pragmatic and doable detail. The way to go is by simplifying matters, always. Now and again, brainpower must be given clear-cut orders. The essence is the Family's. They decide. Therefore they get to choose the smells, music and the favorite color of flowers. There are no two ways about it; it is part of the journey the owners want in place (Table 4.4).[16]

Likewise it was concluded that many interaction messages with clients needed to be industrialized. They could not be left up to each director. The Artemis style had to be defined and industrialized. Industrializing did not mean overlooking closeness and the family atmosphere; it meant giving everybody a script on how to interact. Large hotel chains are experts at that; the example of the Ritz hotels and their client procedures were a baseline (greeting each client when meeting them on the corridor, being ready to help them when needed, welcome/leaving procedure, etc.).

I wish to make a special mention of the sterling work done on the customer journey in the Food & Beverage area.[17] Each hotel went on the F&B journey

---

[16] Harmonizing is hard work. Above all, when actors have been spotting service elements by themselves. My recipe is simple: clear-cut orders, focus and simplicity. And the one in charge gives the orders. Whether it be the owner or CEO. They must act.

[17] F&B is considered one of the most important aspects of client experience in Artemis hotels. Raw material is deemed a priority and they sought to stress this factor.

Table 4.4 Some examples of queries to spawn KPI

Outside entrance	The client's first moment of truth (MT). Materialize five senses essence
Inside entrance	Standard aesthetic design
Physical reception	Question to spot expectations
Five senses	Smell, flowers, tidiness
Checkout	Standard satisfaction question
Billing	Simplicity
Exiting hotel	Escort, question to spot latent demand

along its four facets, which enabled making an overall map for each hotel and the differences between them. Benchmark actions were spotted that could be analyzed and incorporated into every hotel in the group. Much debate was held on clients entering the restaurant and how this interaction should take place. That led to the start of cross-learning between hotels.

An important aspect of the "customer journey" exercise is to get mutual learning and consistency among different Units.[18] Each hotel has its own category and specific services portfolio. The aim was that all should have the same imprint and that a client, in any of them, could distinguish the Artemis hallmark. A group of six hotels, not six hotels with the same owner.

To sum up, the customer journey enables focusing on substantially transmitting the essence by spotting the salient touchpoints. Every agent's action guidelines for client contact must be similar. Standardizing and industrializing is a very important path for services to follow. Consistently transmitting the essence requires it. A five-star service must entail industrialized action to help solve problems as efficiently as possible. Artemis has begun to understand this in its quest to transmit its essence in every fiber of its service.

It Is Not a Quality Problem: Clients Become a Headache When There Are No Clear Service Specifications

Achilles had spotted service problems with certain clients that were giving them multiple headaches. G12 widely debated whether conflicts arose due to the client archetype, or whether they were down to another unidentified component. Lack of consensus over the diagnosis led to starting up a customer journey to spot the troublesome TPs.

---

[18] Journeys were also undertaken with each hotel's overall service in mind.

The journey showed that the problem was not so much the way the TPs unfolded, but was much broader. The client archetypes worked well enough and what looked like a service problem was not.

Customer relations problems had been encompassed as quality problems when really they were not. Customers demanded action that had not been specified, and the agreed service on offer had gaps in it that the customer's imagination could fill in with troublesome requests. A broader analysis of the journey that added a more overall SPDM view enabled understanding that it was not a matter of customers' quirks, but a problem with service specification. If there was no clear-cut specification, reliability could not be measured and everything was left up to the customer's subjective view. And to that were added some customers' unreal (quasi-fanciful) expectations.[19] This leads to very dangerous situations for the margin, as the customer is totally insatiable and asks, and asks, relentlessly.

The situation is simple, as such. The more abstract the specification, the more demands the customer can make afterward. Less specification, more fantasy. This translates into headaches, lower margin, time wasted in endless phone calls at any time of day, and reprocesses. And totally irritated brainpower that makes service interactions terribly fraught. To cap it all, the certification and control area was raising many expectations due to lack of service reliability and it seemed the Achilles Promise was not being kept.

This situation needed urgently tidying up and specifying. The control area could provide valuable information to enable learning from compliance/deviation in each agreed service. This would help polish up future specifications. Service breakdowns were not breakdowns; they were unsuitable specifications and service design. All the more so if there were delays between tabling and signing proposals, because that allowed clients to keep making requests for which there was no place anymore.

Solving this situation at Achilles demanded setting up a project called Client Specifications Implementation (CSI), which would have to work in step with I-CAN and TREASURE. Given that the project meant involving many areas in Achilles, G12 detailed one of its components, María, as the person with authority and drive to push through CSI. In an impeccable job led by María, CSI has become the method for developing the process for specifying and contracting a service at Achilles.

---

[19] Remember; the customer is frivolous, whimsical, vindictive and spiteful. But the customer is king.

Initially, CSI spotted the following problems.[20]

- Lack of detail of the service required by the client
- Downtime due to lack of communication between different agents
- Lack of process structuring and efficiency
- Lack of an intermediate agent between different managers involved and the client
- Lack of consistent criteria to follow to determine, assess and size up the service
- Renegotiations and changes to the contract signing process

The list of problems was the starting point for the work to be done by the group. A novel aspect of CSI cropped up when María decided to build her own area of experts, "area 20". She asked each department who their specialists were in relevant issues and used that information to create a group she dubbed "area 20". This area was made up of wise men to call on whenever CSI needed data on whether Achilles had specific knowledge that should be located in a fresh proposition. Remember that Achilles used its Transformation Plan as a cornerstone in using knowledge. And clearly in CSI one needs to know who knows what, and what they know. Services are being set and that requires having such information at one's fingertips.

Area 20 is a patchwork solution. But a necessary solution until TREASURE comes up with the knowledge database (or KDB) needed for CSI and Achilles. The KDB starts with I-CAN and TREASURE develops it. The overall idea is that when a client asks for a new service, one that has not been on offer before, CSI should spot who has the knowledge needed (or who has the potential to develop it). This way, the ability to provide the service on offer fits in with a swift assessment of the proposition's feasibility.

CSI methodology, currently up and running, entails the following measures:

- *CSI touchpoint.* Introduce a new agent whose basic duties are coordinator/ monitor, to become the TP between client and Achilles.
- *Service scope.* Checklist based on the 4W & H to determine the service's required scope (Table 4.5).
- *Criteria.* Developing criteria for all requests based on the following:

---

[20] They have been voiced by Achilles, but could actually belong to any company. Do they not sound familiar to you?

Table 4.5 4W & H

What	What business area does it affect?
	Client types
	Service types
	Service description
	Nature of service
	Partial or complete service?
	Volumes
	Required service-level indicators
	Additional service follow-up required?
When	When does service start?
	Is there a regulatory deadline or do they set a date for us?
	Service periodicity
	Service working hours
	Length of service
Why	Reason for requesting service
Who	Knowledge needed
How	Technology and/or third-party backup

- Ability to provide service or possibility to acquire it (knowledge and tools).
- Feasibility to give our areas service or extend to existing clients.
- Possibility of extending Achilles' services portfolio.

• Service *Design Team*. Set up Service Design team to streamline the CSI flow, backed up by Area 20, to break down the innovative service into known modules.
• Indicators. KPI and SLA, while fully negotiating all aspects of the service.

Implementing the CSI has not been trouble-free. María said: "What is giving us most trouble is having the proposition include the description of service level indicators that are being weighed up for assessing it. We are in quite a mess, without realizing that adjusting them will impact the service settings and associated costs."

A month into implementing the CSI project and using its methodology for 60% of service requests, María said the following had been learned:

• The checklist, relevant questions to ask the client as well as in-house, is the most important part. Bring up all issues we do not know of, or must bear in mind, in order to implement the service. We have seen cases where a client representative, who was our contact, did not have enough information to clarify the service and that has shown up the need for more complete information. Feedback is important, as well as updates depending on the experience acquired in applying the CSI. Improvements are a must and questions must be thorough when it comes to covering all aspects.

- Speed and materialization are obtained when leading the client by the hand. Help to materialize the service request, while avoiding problems in understanding how the proposal is presented. Likewise, it raises needs we can cover by offering services the client did not know we could offer, or it spots opportunities for extending the perimeter to other related services.
- The whole organization needs CSI training. That enables transmitting CSI's advantages and avoiding service problems.
- Managers must be CSI drivers. No proposition should be made without using CSI. Evidence leads us to understand that that is absolutely necessary, if we are not to slip back into a conflictive situation with clients, as has happened to us.

Sweet talk never convinces; facts do. CSI methodology will be accepted totally when it is shown that using it does away with currently existing problems. It is critical to understand that designing the service settings is the mainstay for defining its specifications, and that customer satisfaction comes with delivering what is promised. The clearer it is, the more KISS it is. And the more KISS, the more efficient.

Looking Again at Servitization

The previous chapter ended with problems a Portuguese company had when it wanted to switch from selling products to selling services. We are now in a position to list the measures that company must take. Tackling so-called servitization requires changing the operations settings and for that the following steps must be taken:

Step 1. Spot the Changes in the Promise's Priorities Services require Promise dimensions that do not usually apply to products. The company must spot the changes in criteria and their assessment. Such prioritization is crucial for step 3.

Step 2. Understand the New Client Archetype Changing from products to services means understanding whether there has been a change in the archetype of the client receiving the service. Hephaestus spotted that a couple of its archetypes did not want to communicate using technology. Nonetheless, as they were not a significant part of service volume, the company carried on with its plans for a technological interface. They could not have done so had the archetype been a significant target for the company. Selling a service entails modifying the concept, but also the way the service is provided for new archetypes that arise.

Step 3. Service Specifications CSI has provided us with a good methodological guide for specifying the service. Getting clients to help define the service as exactly as possible is a critical task when switching from products to services. Clients must understand the changes to, and innovations in, the proposition and their expectations must be materialized as much as possible. Drawing up a checklist provides an industrialized way not to forget any service component, and makes specification reliable.

Step 4. Customer Journey That journey must focus on the service dream and spotting blocking factors that may prevent the new service from being executed. Acting ahead in the customer journey provides a novel view of the difficulties in implementing, and allows them to be smashed at the start, while seeking alternatives for the service settings.

Step 5. Spotting the Knowledge Stock Needed to Solve New Problems that Must Be Tackled The great gap in transformation lies in the knowledge stock needed to tackle the new problems portfolio that will arise. CSI already provides for spotting knowledge types in the services portfolio. But changing from products to services is a change that involves the whole company. We are not talking about one service in particular, but a way of operating a company and its operational priorities. Area 20 was a temporary measure that worked for Achilles. But if we transform to services, we must tackle structural changes. Spotting the knowledge stock needed to solve future problems becomes the mainstay of transformation.

Detecting clients' latent demands must be incorporated alongside these five servitization steps. SPDM holds that in order to spot latent demands (or demand for new provisions, DNP), every agent in the company must know how to observe and listen. I deem this to be a very important factor in servitization, since when a customer relations structure is changed, observing and listening opens the door to spotting actual or future new needs. Spotting them enables new services portfolios to be drawn up. The services innovation cycle (SIC) provides the link between DNP and spawning new services. All the concepts mentioned in this paragraph describe part of the services activities sequence (SAS). The SAS is the model to follow when designing the service configuration. I thus deem it important that our Portuguese company should not only follow the five steps, but ponder what SAS it wants, and implement DNP to support its agents in the transformation.

Designing an idea leads nowhere if you don't make it happen. And making it happen entails multiple conflicting situations. The next three chapters consider situations and measures that have arisen in the four companies, in response to the requirements entailed in implementing. We shall introduce new SPDM ideas to solve new complex situations that have arisen[21] these past years in implementation processes.

SPDM Concepts Used in This Chapter

Chapters referred to: 6 and 9

We began the chapter by introducing archetypes as clients' anthropological profiles. Next, we were introduced to this chapter's overriding concept: the customer journey (point I in the Conceptual Appendix). A customer journey analyzes a client archetype's experience by engendering four journey types: the one that actually happens, the one focusing on needs that clients may have, the one we dream of giving the client and the one that spots blocking factors in implementing the needs spotted. Each journey has five components to be analyzed using the touchpoints (TPs) that clients have with the service. The components are as follows:

- *Finds out.* How clients came across the company: spots the market entry points. How did clients find out about the company?
- *Joins.* Describes how people become clients: how they join the service, through what agents and by what means.
- *Uses.* Defines the use clients make of the current service offered, that is, describes how clients relate to the company once they are part of the client portfolio.

---

[21] Some of them totally new. Others already outlined in my last book.

- *Extends.* Specifies how clients find out about additional services the company offers and how to include the latter in their services portfolio. It is important to know how to steer clients' desire to acquire new services and what agents offers the necessary information.
- *Quits*: Details how the TP quits.

That exercise usually spawns a great deal of information. Grouping and organizing it takes method. With this aim in mind, KJ methodology (point II in the Conceptual Appendix) has been introduced, which visually groups the information obtained by forming clusters of issues to be tackled.

The KJ Method (Muñoz-Seca 2017)

The KJ method is a bottom-up approach that starts off by listing concepts that have a common affinity with pictures. Similarity between concepts is not syntactic, that is, using similar words, but semantic, that is, using pictures that suggest similar concepts. The stress on semantics and shunning syntactics is down to acknowledging that language has certain features that inhibit human creativity. The method sets forth that the best way to sum up a sentence's meaning is in the pictures thought up by people reading them, and therefore in order to gage the similarity between two concepts described by propositions, it is enough to compare the pictures that recipients think up. The pictures thought up are based on individual perceptions and may vary from person to person. Two people may think up totally different pictures when perceiving the same fact.

The knowledge database (KDB) (point III in the Conceptual Appendix), and drawing it up, is another SPDM concept broached in this chapter. Previously, when discussing TREASURE in Chap. 2, we saw verb, object, condition (VOC) indexing. Both are closely linked. What is important about a database is ease of access, and VOC provides a KISS approach to do that. A database stores experiences, and solutions to problems and information. That is the way to spot who knows how to solve what problems and what knowledge they have. The correct use of knowledge is an optimal way to maintain and boost the contribution margin. Materializing that knowledge in KDB format streamlines its use.

The chapter's last section introduces the demand for new provisions (DNP) concept. It aims to spot clients' latent demands (point IV in the Conceptual Appendix). DNP is one activity in the service activities sequence, SAS (Fig. 4.4).

Service settings demand analyzing all the SAS activities and implementing the service innovation cycle (SIC). That cycle links latent demand spotted by agents to devising new services.

Service Design

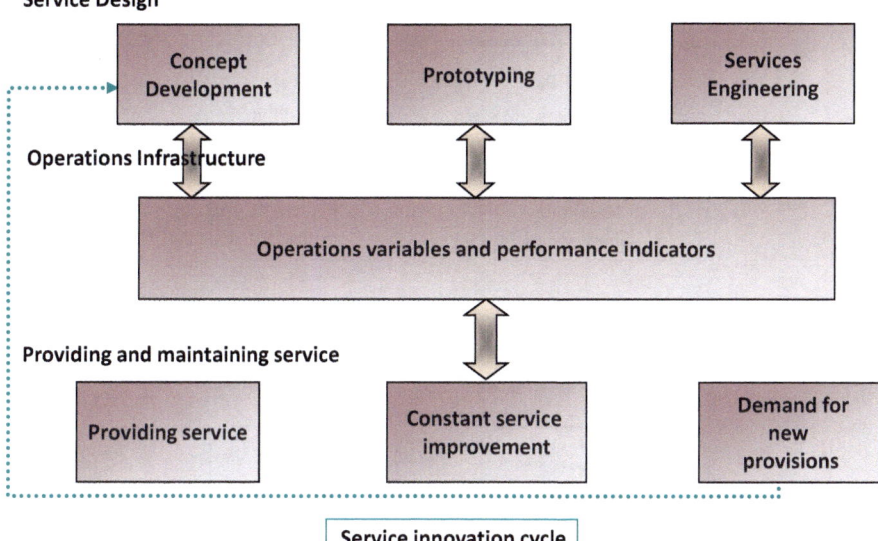

Fig. 4.4   The SAS (Muñoz-Seca 2017)

Chapter 4: Conceptual Appendix

I. Customer journey

	Touchpoint	Know	Involve	Use	Extend	Quit
Reality						
Clients' needs						
Dream we should give them						
Blocking factors						

1. Know: how they know about the service   Good
2. Involve: how they become involved with the service   Bad
3. Use: using the service   N/A
4. Extend: how to channel their desire to acquire other services   Neutral
5. Quit: how the service ends

Know	Involve	Use	Extend	Quit
How did clients find out about the company?	The moment a new client joins the service	What company services do clients use?	What does the current client portfolio need that is not on offer?	Why does a client stop using company services?
Spot a keyword to define the company's service and its essence	What aims does each company agent have?	What do they not use? Why?	What means are made available to clients to boost the number of services they retain?	Is it a natural departure?

II. KJ

Step 1 : Prepare the material	**Step 6 :** Second-level grouping
Step 2: Hand out blank sheets	**Step 7 :** Second-level titles
Step 3 : Jot down problems	**Step 8 :** Compose the panel
Step 4 : Top-level grouping	**Step 9** Separate levels
Step 5 : Top-level titles	**Step 10 :** Differentiate Level 2 & 3

III. KDB

What do I know?	What level do I have?	What do I need to provide five-star service?	Source	How do I get it?	
Knowledge in VOC format	From I to V	VOC from I to V	Who has the knowledge?	I buy	In-company development
Knowledge 1					
Knowledge 2					
Knowledge 3					

IV. Observe and listen to clients' latent demands, or DNP

Checklist for observation and active listening
Pick the team of agents that you will train
Indicate that observation will be part of their normal work and that it will take place in the natural setting where they develop it
Share the Mission's priorities and assessed criteria
Convey the importance of watching out for every detail. Stress client interaction   Apply active listening techniques whenever you are with them

Whenever you are with a client in a situation defined as a "situation of interest":
 	
    Watch out for every detail defined in the observation guide
 	
    Apply active listening techniques at client interaction moments
 	
    Record client's behavior
 	
    Immediately jot down your observations in a notebook
 	
    Afterwards (the same day), pick the most important observations
 	
    Classify, sort or group your observations according to whatever object they refer to
 	
    Use up a single sheet to transcribe the observation once the previous steps have been taken

In direct client interaction:
 	
    Jot down the most important aspects in a notebook, or whatever new questions occur to you
 	
    Connect with client: begin the interaction with general questions so they feel more at ease
 	
    Raise questions to check facts and not to sound out opinions
 	
    Focus on information relating to the present and not the past
 	
    Ask questions that make client share their opinions and analyze the issue more thoroughly
 	
    Raise whatever new questions occur to you in conversation with the interviewee
 	
    Sum up the most important observations and ask if you have understood them properly
 	
    Rewrite your notes right after the interaction to interpret them properly
 	
    Chart data on a graph and draft a written summary of the observation

5

What Shall We Do with the Popups? On-the-Spot Innovation Can Create Unforeseen Problems

Abstract A popup is an innovation that is born of frustration. Service agents see things that do not work and ask for improvements, but the company fails to respond. Their answer is to create an innovation to smash the problem. Such innovations may be excellent, or counterproductive, because while they solve a specific problem they might also do greater damage to the organization as a whole. The chapter shows how to resolve this dilemma, as well as introducing the three agents of innovation (innovator, *innomanager* and *innosufferer*) and showing concrete ways to implement new ideas. It also depicts a hitherto undiagnosed brainpower syndrome, the "Himalayan syndrome".

What is a popup in a company context? By "popup" I mean an innovation sprouting spontaneously to fix a troublesome situation that has not been tackled structurally by the organization. Or to put it plainly: when things go wrong and nobody fixes them, a group takes the initiative, implements a new way to tackle the problem and the rest of the company is none the wiser. Sound familiar? It will to many. We work with brains that have initiative and get fed up with coming across the same old problems it seems nobody wants to solve. As they are forced to deal day in, day out, with a particular snag, they come up with a different way to solve problems that arise. And that is a popup. It does not enter the company's structured channels. It pops up as on a computer screen. Suddenly and by surprise. You see them pop up in a company.

What to do? Management has two options when facing a popup. On the one hand, root it out. On the other, understand why it pops up, what difficulties have made it pop up and spot what formal measures can be taken.

© The Author(s) 2019
B. Muñoz-Seca, *How to Get Things Right*, IESE Business Collection,
https://doi.org/10.1007/978-3-030-14088-5_5

Written like that, it looks like I want to steer readers toward the second option. Indeed, on paper it looks like the one that makes most sense, since it brings about improvement and in-company learning. And with that approach we shall introduce it. But do not underestimate the first option. At times, brainpower needs clear-cut measures to send a straightforward message that a line defining best practice in the company has been crossed. I do not champion drastic measures at all, but brains need to be well aware when they overstep the mark. Any amount of discussion is allowed, but seeking solutions behind the organization's back may be dangerous. Solidifying popups is tantamount to solidifying a malfunction using a temporary solution that becomes structural. A popup is a symptom that something is not right. And as such, it must be studied, analyzed and observed. But a solidified popup may be a terrible setback to a company's regular functioning.

Pegasus was in that situation. One of the company's areas decided that it would solve problems independently and devised its own procedures, software and operations. Behind the rest of the company's back, without telling the Organization department, IT, nobody. In their own way and using their own know-how, which was very broad. Such coteries may add huge value to a company or provide endless headaches. Handling and keeping tabs on them is an indispensable preventive job in companies these days.[1] The Pegasus group was an association of highly qualified brains, with all a brainpower's features raised to the nth degree. Setting up independent republics for action/knowledge without bearing in mind the rest of the organization is one thing they tend to do. And of course, they spawn popups.

Let us not confuse this approach with setting up Knowledge Units (KUs).[2] That is something completely different. A popup is reactive, a KU proactive. A popup is a quick fix, a KU a structural grouping to help solve exploratory problems in the rest of the company.

What happened at Pegasus? Well they had to root out the solidified popup, people left and productivity fell. It took a lot of work, perseverance and patience to set up a sustainable and efficient solution. A "we do it ourselves" group operations culture entails solutions that bring only partial—not overall—benefits. And often an endemic malaise for the organization.

Bearing in mind the aforesaid, let us now analyze proposals for rooting out as well as building from a popup.

---

[1] I do not wish to repeat what my last book said. If readers are interested, please go to Chapter 8 in my book *How to Make Things Happen*, Palgrave Macmillan, 2017.
[2] We shall discuss Knowledge Units in the next chapter.

Rooting Out Popups

Scenario: a popup has sprouted and is diagnosed as a solution not in keeping with the company, as it solves an occasional problem but provides no sustainable solution for the Organization.

Proposed solution: root it out forthwith, that is, overnight, but use the knowledge derived to make the agents who built the popup come up with alternatives within the company framework.

How to Carry that Out

Overnight is a very drastic solution that requires some preparation. Hurry as we might, it is better to take the odd break.

One of Artemis's hotel managers had been working for the company for years. A capacity analysis (see Chap. 3) found that his administrator was the most efficient one. That allowed the director to comply fully with the requisite 50% time outside the office. On paper, and coldly, everything looked fine. But it was not so.

Problem? Popups were a high percentage of the hotel's functioning. Ad hoc solutions Artemisia was unaware of and that had been implemented for years, and unbeknown specifically to the rest of the company.

After looking into what was going on, what procedures were used, how he worked with his administrator, what he knew, and sundry other diagnoses, the manager was asked for structured measures. He was asked to devise, along with tiers in the central organization, procedures and protocols to materialize the knowledge his hotel had developed. The aim was that Artemis as a whole should benefit from what had been learned in said hotel.

Like a good brainpower, the manager never looked for trouble, but for twists and turns instead to keep doing what he thought best. And so it was, it was good for his hotel, but his way of doing things lost Artemis as a whole a lot of value. Remember that the Artemis Family owners wanted six hotels with the same essence.

How did they cope with rooting out the popup? The biggest existing concern was losing knowledge stock and not benefiting from the popups involved in running his hotel. But clearly things could not stay that way. The Family did not want each hotel to work as it sought fit.[3] It wanted to take advantage of all the wealth of latent learning in Artemis that had not been materialized for general use.

---

[3] Albeit with the best of intentions and in agreement with some Family member or other. But this unilateral approach is not only unsustainable, but very risky. Knowledge is in a few people's heads; it is not shared around and does not lead to sustainability.

The solution arose by chance. Another hotel manager left Artemis, and it was decided that the aforementioned manager should take over running that hotel as well. Upon so doing, he was obliged to spell out and materialize his way of operating so that Artemis could learn from it, and make the treasured lessons available to everybody.

Can we deem this example a suitable way to root out a popup? Well I think so. When the manager had to run two hotels at once, he had no choice but to materialize his know-how using processes and procedures. A win-win situation. He won, Artemis won. Likewise, operations rules and criteria for prioritizing had to be materialized in order to share them, as the manager could not be in two places at once and had to formalize his way of proceeding so agents could take decisions in his absence. All this learning, together with small service details that had been designed to safeguard the essence[4] the Family had conveyed to him, was incorporated into other hotels and led to much joint learning.

At Pegasus, the popup's builders left the company and made way for readjustment. But this is not the "No Hire, No fire" way, since much value added knowledge and experience was lost.[5] Rooting out often entails complicated concomitant situations that are totally unnecessary. Spotting popups when they first appear is essential, because rooting them out then is not very traumatic, and opens the way to improvement. Pegasus has been suffering the consequences of rooting out popups for more than one year and a half.[6]

Learning and Using Popups as a Prototype

Scenario: a popup has appeared and been diagnosed as a solution for an occasional problem that requires thorough understanding and an integral—possibly industrializable—solution.

Proposed solution: turn popups into prototypes, a source of learning and the way to standardize by feeding improvement dynamics.

How to Carry that Out

A company area spots a problematic situation and takes a unilateral decision to act individually. That usually stays hidden, as the area has little interest in broadcasting it so as not to cause trouble.

---

[4] The type of napkins they used and how they folded them, the way clients were welcomed in the dining room, check-in details and so on, and so forth.

[5] Obviously, by that time the popup was truly enormous.

[6] And with much suffering on many sides. Only perseverance and constant work by some has managed to remedy the situation.

Management catches wind of it from some interaction or comment. And proposes it as a prototype.[7] In consequence, the area is asked to take basic prototyping steps, among others:

- Understand its fundamental purpose
- Understand what functionality is sought after
- Learn from mistakes in implementation
- Improve
- Reassess again
- T2: try and train
- Implement
- Industrialize

As required by these measures, the area had no choice but to use all its experience and know-how to create/validate the prototype.

Transforming a popup into a prototype requires methodology and time to act. Normally, a popup is a quick fix, born of frustration over a continuing malfunction. And prototyping is not quick. For that reason I recommend[8] applying all the principles of rapid prototyping[9] (Brown and Wyatt 2010) and lean start-up (Ries[10] 2011). These techniques drive deft prototyping and compress time to speed up implementation.

Every project we saw at Achilles had the prototype format and was a peerless source of learning for the company. They were used to show how one area's know-how was unknown in another. Remember that investing time in finding solutions to problems that are already known is an endless source of inefficiency. Time must be invested in new problems, while known ones must be industrialized and standardized.

Prototyping is a great way for companies to learn, and it creates an important knock-on effect. Achilles has been there with I-CAN and TREASURE. Their prototypes were redefined; they spread throughout the company and thoroughly transformed agents' everyday work. Proving a situation empirically is much more effective than a thousand words.[11]

---

[7] Prototyping is one activity in the SAS design chain, introduced in the previous chapter.

[8] For more details, see Chapter 9 in my book *How to Make Things Happen*.

[9] Rapid prototyping, a design thinking approach. At the core of the implementation process is the prototype, converting ideas into actual services that are then tested, repeated and perfected.

[10] Get several practices going that shorten the product development cycle, measure actual progress without resorting to complicated indicators and help to understand what clients really want.

[11] And that is this book's fundamental purpose. I hope that voicing the four companies' actual SPDM experiences will help to implement them in many others.

Popups May Appear Because Innovations Are Not Foreseen When Needed to Implement Improvements

Prototyping helps to understand whether a company has enough know-how to tackle the implementation problems that will arise. It acts like a catalyst five minutes ahead, as it enables simulating implementation. It helps shorten the implementation distance for new ideas, and to spot know-how that has to be developed or extended.

When this does not happen, popups may appear to produce the innovations needed to implement ideas. They might be small innovations[12] that go along with the aim of solving minor problems due to implementation. Ad hoc changes that may not seem worth requesting a structural change in the way of proceeding, and are sorted out using popups that then solidify and spawn inefficiency. And therein lies the problem.[13]

While Pegasus worked to compress time, a special group was set up to take charge of implementing proposals in the extended enterprise. The work groups devised measures that would come to fruition in the extended enterprise, not Pegasus. This particular group was dubbed the "Implementation Coaches". It was not an intervention group. Its main purpose was to prevent problems and act five minutes ahead of possible conflictive situations that implementation might mean for the extended enterprise. They had to warn each extended enterprise of the possible particular effects that the proposed measures would have on their company. The aim was that each extended enterprise, with its own idiosyncrasies, could take suitable measures that would allow it to digest the forthcoming changes.

The theory was impeccable: the extended enterprises would have to modify their way of proceeding. A tsunami of measures came their way, which could be taken on when tackled with a preventive and planned approach, but absent prevention, they could lead to deadlock or thousands of popups appearing as stopgap measures. This would lead to no wealth of intra/inter-extended learning; each situation would be seen as novel and the learning curve would be nonexistent. An unproductive nightmare.

---

[12] So-called creeping innovations or, by extension, which arise to fix structured high- or low-variety problems.

[13] I must make clear that I do not champion totally structuring/materializing every little innovation, as that can lead to straight-jacketing and deadlock. But they must be spotted and revised periodically to see how much they are used, as well as their value added. That functioning must be adopted structurally and handed to the manager in charge of the project as part of the latter's daily work. Innovations used sporadically and that have no great impact may well stay put, but they must be known. Those that enhance performance or entail solutions that may have a novel impact on other areas must be analyzed to be industrialized afterwards.

As readers know well, theory is one thing, and practice, another. And this idea failed in practice. The coaches received suitable operational knowledge for diagnosing possible future problems in the extended enterprise. They were routinely briefed about every modification that was in the pipeline and those that were approved. A track was devised to evacuate operating problems that cropped up, that is, a special problem-solving fast track for the latter. It was all immaculate and those in charge of the Time Compression project were wholly dedicated.

Why do I deem it a failure? Well, for the simple reason that the preventive message was not driven home. The coaches' everyday work was so focused on solving daily operational problems that they could not see the wood for the trees. They were incapable of glimpsing the total significance of the need to preventively assess the extended enterprise. Result? The measures were implemented along with all the necessary regulations, but with ad hoc adjustments. Stopgaps, in other words. They have been since modified, but by bit, to cull learning. Therefore, reprocessing. If the coaches had analyzed each measure's potential impact on each extended enterprise company, this situation would not have arisen.[14]

Let us distinguish between popups and such stopgaps arising. Stopgaps are caused when no preventive action has been taken to query the problems that may arise when innovations are implemented. A popup is a response to an undiagnosed situation that arises and must be fixed quickly. But not preventing problems in implementing innovations is inefficient. Let us not confuse matters. Popups are ideas arising with a "guerrilla" mindset, not mentioned in the rulebook, to tackle a repetitive inefficiency situation the organization does not fix. Lack of foresight is a dysfunction that must not be tolerated. Stopgaps are inefficient and do not get to the bottom of the problem. They do not fix, they seek compromise. And in Operations they are usually dismal.

What has been learned from the Pegasus situation? Well, we must look at Achilles' I-CAN project and its 10 lessons. Methodological drivers do a very good job in helping groups understand the impact I-CAN can have on their workaday way of operating. And that entails groups seeing what is in it for them. At Pegasus, we did not know how to do that, did not know how to convey the impact the tsunami could have on the coaches' workaday duties. Maybe because it was extensive and seen from afar. Maybe because the daily grind stopped them looking up, and they felt they had not unlocked capacity to deal with it.[15] Achilles, meanwhile, did unlock capacity to execute the I-CAN plans and did help to understand I-CAN's usefulness when helping to rationalize their workday jobs.

---

[14] Or it would have been minimized.

[15] Although they performed a capacity analysis, the mismatch was seen in the consumption and tasks they had; they tried to standardize and cut consumption. Some of them did learn from it and applied the lessons to their duties and the extended enterprise. Others did not.

Paradoxically, Pegasus has its flame red in the extended enterprise and its functioning is critical to making things happen. There is no true implementation without the extended enterprise acting. Nonetheless, they did not know how to convey the impact a preventive action could have on speeding up implementation.

By comparing both actions, at Pegasus and Achilles, we understand the need to materialize the actual impact before beginning any preventive action. Holding dry runs of what may happen is a good way to make those involved understand the looming reality.

Summing up. Let us distinguish between popups and stopgaps. Popups must be transformed into prototypes for sustained improvement. Stopgaps must be treated as a failure to prevent an implementation's consequences. They must be rooted out and transformed into structural changes.

The Himalaya Syndrome

A behavior pattern that may be confused with popups is the Himalaya syndrome.[16] It consists of having very brainy, very competent, very knowledgeable brains that are fed up with the organization not responding as deftly as they would like, and that decide to do their own thing, by asking third parties for measures and resources, according to their own service design. They are usually very efficient, hard-working and decisive brains.

The conflict lies in their view that only what they set up is the way to get results.[17] The existing situation adds no value. The diagnosis may be right, but the way they go about fixing the situation is "my way". They are one-man adjustments to the existing situation, modifying details or side-stepping measures they deem irrelevant. They are different to popups in that they are not structured or integral solutions. They modify part of the process in the company's workaday functioning.

At Pegasus we worked with a Himalaya brain. Brilliant. He had been entrusted with a hard job and decided the regular way would not help him meet the set goals. And he had to act. He accepted the *autoritas* of those whom he saw knew more than him in other areas. But for him, the rest were irrelevant. They had given him a job to do, and come what may, he would get it done.

Great patience and much perseverance got him to understand that the service design's fullest outlines, as shown him, would achieve the same results. But by working together. And this job would also require many changes, but

---

[16] Alludes to believing themselves on top of the world.

[17] And they are often right.

changes already adapted to full functioning. It required constant consensus, but that was the way to get good results.

Working with Himalaya syndromes requires constant negotiation. But it is worthwhile. Brilliant brains are impatient and despise inefficiency. They must be shown that their way adds no sustainability to the company. It is well known that this requires getting across practicalities, bit by bit.

Achilles also had a Himalaya manager. He chose the ideas that best fitted in with his work, adapted them after his own fashion and off he went. Made to measure. The rest of G12 did not mind, as they all knew he was a loner and that his way of doing things had gotten good results in other instances. His participating in G12 contributed a different view on many situations, although it must be said that at times they had to get him back on track.[18]

Working with him[19] was focused on sharing lessons he had learned from implementing ideas in the whole Transformation Plan. As part of G12, another three group members joined him in developing a methodological summary of his working practices. They sat with him, asked him, queried him, learned, added, modified them and devised a methodological proposal to include it in the Transformation Plan. It was then being implemented in an area under a G12 member, in the prototype phase to spot complete methodological feasibility and adjust the design. Two G12 members were becoming trainers and executors of the methodology devised in order to implement it in other Achilles departments. It is an iterative process requiring constant work. It started from an individualistic premise, and has been joined to solid conceptual ideas to turn it into methodology for the plan. Knowledge has been culled and materialized to make it available throughout Achilles.

The Innosufferer's Role[20]

One of the biggest blockages that appears in implementing measures is some brains' refusal to cooperate and change. There are many reasons and all come under "resistance to change". As we all know, we can have no resistance. Plain fear of not being up to it, of not knowing how to solve new problems, of facing the unknown.

---

[18] Remember that only autoritas (the authority somebody has by themselves, regardless of their institutional role in the company) achieves this. Himalayas do not believe in potestas (power invested in somebody due to the position they hold in the company).

[19] This Himalaya will be a Himalaya until he retires. But what he does gets results, so a way must be found to fit him in and benefit from his developments.

[20] Remember the three roles in implementing innovation: innovator, innomanager and innosufferer. The latter is on the receiving end of innovation, the one that executes it.

Achilles immediately spotted this potential blockage and G12 introduced an innosufferer, Ana, who took full responsibility for her role. She was the voice of the people and behaved like it. Ana was accompanied by two other innosufferers, but she took on the claimant's role. The idea came from the Achilles CEO, who had foreseen that implementing the plan would be a major challenge, and wanted to spot potential blockages preventively.

At the start of the project, Ana realized that a major blocking factor was the vocabulary to be used in transmitting ideas and aims. She forbade certain words due to the mistaken messages they might send, and asked for terms to be clarified when they were to be used. A large part of the staff became innosufferers and had to understand clearly the concepts that would be handled along with the ideas to be transmitted. Ana would not tolerate misinterpreting messages and, therefore, strove to clarify everything as much as possible. She had seen lack of clarity before and wanted no more of it.

The Achilles CEO granted Ana much authority. When there was a problem with some implementation, she was summoned swiftly to help understand where the troublesome situation had its cause. We might think this situation gave her airs, but not a bit of it. Her personal attitude was proactive and helpful at all times. A very hard-working woman, Ana was the first to test novel ideas in her projects and spot troublesome issues before others.

Every G12 project came under Ana's watchful eye, whose mainstay was how to fit the 700 into the Achilles plan. In this role she acted as consultant to every project, so that they were seen from the perspective of the brain that was to implement them, and to spot such blockages as might be caused. Acting five minutes ahead became a constant variable in her approach, as she tried to understand the effect measures would have on those involved.

But Ana was not just a star innosufferer that warned of risks. As an active G12 member she led her project at Achilles.

That function has only appeared at Achilles. Pegasus had its implementation coaches in the extended enterprise that we have seen. Hephaestus had totally reconciled the idea of potential blockages if they did not consider innosufferers, and their smaller size did not require such a function, as Achilles did.

At Artemis, the blockages would not arise in regular staff but hotel managers. They were the ones that felt their workaday role threatened and they constituted a blocking force. Therefore, it is essential to distinguish between innosufferers as recipients of the innovation and managers that want to block the measure because it attacks their area of influence and power. They are totally different issues, but both hinder implementation.[21]

---

[21] I believe managers that do not want to play should be clear about what their future is. They will find pastures anew.

Incorporating innosufferers requires making them participate in the problem's causality, giving them options for action and to jointly understand that adjacent situations occur that have not been analyzed, because the view has not been that of those that do things, but a more overall one. Joining overall and micro views like this is absolutely indispensable to make implementation work.

There are times when an innomanager begins their action plan with some specific aims. But these become distorted because the innosufferer comes up with unsuspected situations that modify the approach. That is what happened to Ana in her role as innomanager.

Ana wanted to start a cursory analysis with her team of the knowledge needed to devise new jobs, as I-CAN was planned for a distant time slot. She floated questionnaires for her work team following SPDM methodology to analyze knowledge by adapting its vocabulary and meaning (Table 5.1).[22]

Ana could make no progress with them, because the multiple efficiency problems that arose were such that they had to be focused on, while leaving aside the knowledge needs.

Ana immediately diagnosed the problems with the situation and understood that inefficiency allowed for no progress. But that did not bother her. Inefficiency causes frustration and the latter should go away, so that knowledge needs might arise that are required to tackle today's and tomorrow's problems. It took just a bit of calm reflection using methodology to make problems surface that had been ingrained for some time, and nobody had tackled. Ana understood that she had to keep up with her innosufferers, because otherwise she would not reach her targets.

Table 5.1 SPDM format for extracting knowledge and Ana's translation

SPDM format				
Activity	What problems do you come across?	What decision do you take?	Why do you take it?	Personal criteria for decision-taking
How Ana translated for her group				
Activity	How do you do your activity?	What problems do you come across?	What decisions do you take?	

---

[22] Another Achilles G12 member has devised their own personal version of these SPDM questions. He has paraphrased them by asking: How do you do it? What problems do you come across? What decisions do you make? What limitations do you find for more business?

Innosufferers block implementation when they take no part in improvement, and have no chance to allow inefficiencies to surface in implementation proposals. It is a response to impotence. And if they do not block it, they may devise popups to tackle problems that they have had no chance to report. If you do not want popups, involve innosufferers to make them see the problems portfolio from their own standpoint. Or allow popups to arise on the understanding that their life cycle must be minimal and in the knowledge that you are allowing them to arise. Movement is important; solidifying, harmful.

Finally, do not stifle brains' ability to contribute different ways of proceeding. Steer that strength through channels by giving them special paths. They are a great investment and must not be squandered.

SPDM Concepts Used in This Chapter

Chapters referred to: 9 and 15

The chapter's title focuses its message on a new concept: popups. A popup describes the need to devise an innovation to fix a dysfunctional situation that nobody can or wants to fix. The idea of popups has surfaced over these past three years of implementation in observing such situations in some companies, in those analyzed in this book as well as others.

Using popups as prototypes is an SPDM approach and fits in with the SAS described in the previous chapter. A popup belongs to the service dream area and must be understood as a one-off group effort to fix the odd situation.

To understand popups is to understand the innovation process and an innosufferer's role. Three roles exist when implementing any innovation (point I in the Conceptual Appendix).

- Innovator: an agent that introduces the innovation to the company
- Innomanager: an agent in charge of making the innovation succeed
- Innoreceiver (innosufferer): an agent that ends up suffering or noticing the innovation's effects on their work

An innovation's success depends, to a great extent, on the way each one is assigned a role according to the job they do (point II in the Conceptual Appendix). When it comes to implementing, each of these actors must receive a specific/different type of support for the process to succeed.

Table 5.2 Brainpower's attributes (Muñoz-Seca 2017)

All they have is their knowledge and they feel proud of it. They are proud of having achieved the targets set and find their efforts must be appreciated by society
They think their boss does not understand the situation. They will never think their boss gets it right. They will always think they could do it much better and the boss understands neither the concept nor the situation
They are very aware of what is happening around them. They put up personally with the organization's inefficiencies and feel frustrated at not being able to provide the optimal solution
They have sized up everybody else very well. Without making value judgments, they are very aware of everybody's abilities and what they are suited to
They cultivate their identity, and seek to stand out. They need to feel unique, different
They accept autoritas, *but not* potestas. They will not compromise with *potestas.* Do not force solutions on them, give them problems
They require consistent and clear pitches. They do not need to agree with the company's strategy, but they must understand why it has been devised and the path the company will follow

Not relying on the innovation recipient's attributes and needs prevents making action plans happen. They simply do not see the light of day. Intertwined with this idea is the concept that we work with brainpower. And brainpower has very significant attributes.[23] Table 5.2 sums them up.

Finally, innovating spawns problems. We must distinguish between spawning structured and unstructured problems.

Structured	Those that may be solved by applying a sequence of operations, or problem-solving process. Solutions to such problems will come with an applicable solution process
Unstructured	Those for which, a priori, it is impossible to find what solutions are satisfactory. Solutions to such problems will come with an exploratory solution process

For unstructured or unknown problems, the solution process is by searching (or exploratory). For structured or known problems, the solution process is by knowledge application. The two must be clearly distinguished. Managers must know whether their contributors have the knowledge stock to face the problems assigned them in a known fashion, or by trial and error. Both solution processes are very disparate. And when acting on a known problem, exploring is most inefficient. Time and effort are wasted. And it is very frustrating (Table 5.3).

---

[23] For more on this issue, see Chapter 7 of my book *How to Make Things Happen*, which is wholly dedicated to managing brainpower.

Table 5.3 Two types of solution process (Muñoz-Seca 2017)

Exploration	Application
Takes much time	Quick
May be frustrating	May be simple
Guarantees no results by a deadline	Guarantees short-term results
Enables learning	Adds information and experience
Room for creativity	Not much is learned
Enables finding unprecedented solutions	Nothing new is obtained
Trial and error	

Chapter 5: Conceptual Appendix

I. Each agent's role

	Agree ✓	Doubtful x
Innovator		
In charge of implementing the new way of proceeding?		
Must they bear in mind the innovation's effect before it is implemented?		
Do they have *autoritas*?		
Innomanager		
In charge of ensuring problems pose d by implementation are absorbed by innoreceivers?		
In charge of maximizing innoreceivers' learning during the process?		
Line manager?		
Innosufferer		
Must they implement the innovation?		
Must they respond to problems posed by innovation?		
Active subject in the learning process?		

II. Innovation agents

Spotting innovation agents		
Innovator	Innomanager	Innosufferer
Agent introducing innovation	*Agent(s) in charge of making innovation succeed*	*Agents suffering effects of innovation on workaday duties*
Agent 1:	Agent 1:	Agent 1:
	Agent 2:	Agent 2:
		Agent 3:

6

The Five-Star Constellation and Knowledge Pills

Abstract The Five-Star Constellation blends capacity analysis with spotting the knowledge stock required to solve today's and tomorrow's problems. A knowledge pill is a focused training concept for a very particular set of tasks. It usually comes in two- to three-minute YouTube video clips. This chapter shows how our companies have implemented such concepts. Setting up "knowledge units" is also shown as a way to achieve sustainable efficiency.

Cristina, HR manager at Hephaestus, was mulling over the ongoing transformation in the Emergency Unit. Her department was in charge of driving and monitoring the capacity analysis, because Hephaestus's size made it more reasonable for HR to do so. HR's message regarding the capacities analysis had been: "The more transparent and honest we are about capacities analysis, the sooner we can table solutions to achieve operational efficiency."

Work done had shown how to improve consumption, and new secondary tasks opened the way to adding value to the coordinators' duties. Hephaestus is a very gas-focused company and the sought-after transformation to a customer focus required adding new tasks, in order to offer new services. The challenge was to set up a Hephaestus 4.0 by paraphrasing the messages sent by the digital transformation inherent in Industry 4.0.

Cristina drew up a list of lessons learned by HR after coordinating the capacity analysis in Emergency and other Hephaestus departments. The salient points were:

- The capacity analysis translates into professional and personal growth by cutting inefficiencies.

© The Author(s) 2019
B. Muñoz-Seca, *How to Get Things Right*, IESE Business Collection,
https://doi.org/10.1007/978-3-030-14088-5_6

- Some capacities are unsuited to the jobs assigned.
- Value-added activities are not performed because tasks that add little value consume resources.
- The team is used to neither internal analysis nor querying their activities' status quo. This "unrest" must be empowered.
- We need everybody behind the criteria for action.
- We need to know how to dream of an ideal operational world.
- We have to formalize informal tasks.

Capacity analysis has made its mark and the CEO has been a major driver. The CEO had asked each department to think things over after the capacity exercise, and suggested three things to them:

1. What they must do to cut consumption and be more efficient.
2. What they would use the unlocked capacity for.
3. Spell out their operating dream to see if they needed new knowledge stock.

For example, Hephaestus's Billing area, whose occupancy rate was nearly 100%, had answered as follows:

1. How can I be more efficient?

   - By cutting time spent on tasks such as complaints and spending it instead on others with greater added value
   - By industrializing accountancy staff
   - By outsourcing printing, enveloping and mailing

2. Lowering the current occupancy rate will enable extracting brains' potential for:

   - Analyzing clients/grids/detours/consumption

3. Operating dream?

   - Doing verification work to enhance quality in billing
   - Spreading billing jobs and knowledge
   - Cutting complaints rate to 10%
   - Individual billing on domestic market, thus eliminating aggregate billing and jobs required
   - Automating billing
   - Electronic billing to eliminate mailing paper bills

Capacity analysis had made a soft landing at Hephaestus, as it is a concrete and rational issue. Meanwhile, operations issues like interruptions and reprocesses had been likewise assimilated perfectly. It was a good job, ideas began to flow.

Cristina was satisfied, but knew she had to go one step beyond. They had to delve into knowledge. HR had spotted that critical knowledge was concentrated in a few people. And that was dangerous for Hephaestus. Cristina had enthusiastically accepted the problem = knowledge approach. She saw the need to rationalize the use of knowledge and what would be needed to face tomorrow's problems. She wanted to come up with a hefty pitch about knowledge to persuade her current ecosystem, composed of PI, grid infrastructure and technical matters. "This knowledge stuff sounds very airy-fairy to them," Cristina thought. "They don't think it's very practical. They tell me it's HR baloney, no use at all. How do I convince them?"

An answer was needed to Cristina's question. It was imperative to spread knowledge needed for today and spot/develop that needed for tomorrow. Hephaestus's transformation project needed to incorporate knowledge.

A few days later, I lay on the grass to gaze at the stars.[1] The sky was clear and I could see them fully. Mulling over the narrative Cristina needed and gazing at the lovely, starry sky, I saw the light. Each star was a Hephaestus brain and what we had before us was a Constellation[2] of stars, each with its quirks, but part of a distinguished whole. What is the Constellation composed of? Let us follow Fig. 6.1 to understand what each star and its surroundings are composed of.

- On the one hand, the occupancy rate composed of each person's primary and secondary tasks. We were interested in the primaries, since the secondaries could be replanned and reorganized.
- To execute primaries each star has its knowledge stock for solving today's problems. In the Emergency Unit, we saw how different agents took different times to do similar tasks. The cause and knowledge each agent had was being examined, which enabled them to do their job in the most efficient way while keeping up the level of service.
- New secondary activities would require new knowledge stock, since they consisted of an unknown tasks portfolio and each agent needed to fill their individual knowledge gaps. Tomorrow's problems had to be solved.

---

[1] Readers might wonder: "She gazes at the stars and thinks about a gas company?" I know it may not sound very inspiring, but I was obsessed with helping Cristina. And when I am obsessed with something, I am like a machine that does not let up. Until I have an answer, my brain sidelines any other matter.

[2] According to the dictionary: Group of stars that, using imaginary lines, forms a picture that evokes a particular figure.

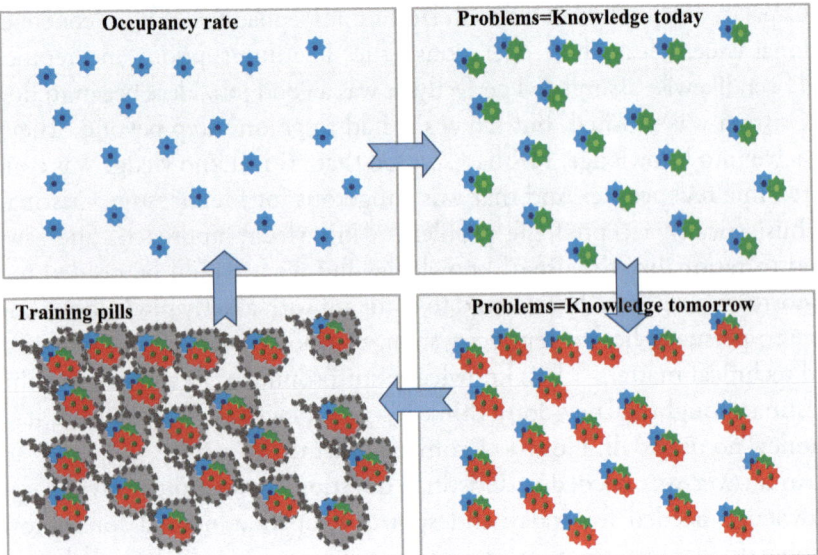

Fig. 6.1 Five-star Constellation

- Acquiring such new knowledge had to focus on knowledge pills. Ad hoc training for ad hoc problems.[3] Benchmark consumption agents were the baseline. Pills would transfer the knowledge to the other agents to cut consumption and unlock capacity. The unlocked capacity would be used to learn new tasks.

An implementation triumvirate was set up, three basic components joined together: occupancy rate, problems and knowledge, and filling knowledge gaps with pills. The Constellation virtuous circle. Unlocking capacity via consumption enables restarting the cycle, since compressing consumption times by using constant learning spurs improvement dynamics.

The narrative began to take shape. We would not mention knowledge in the abstract. We would focus on each individual's triumvirate. And we would call it the "five-star Constellation", since it was a group of agents united by a Promise to deliver an optimal, five-star service.

Next day I called Cristina, and after I told her about my epiphany, she said: "'I'll phrase it in my terms.' Each person at the company does their job using up different times. We want everybody to learn from those who do things in less time, but of course while keeping up the quality of service. That will free up time for people. That free time can be spent doing new things in each department and that transform Hephaestus into a 4.0, and

---

[3] Remember what Chap. 2 said. Pills no more than two minutes long and on video.

make everybody learn and enhance their employability. And for everybody to learn to do things in less time and do new jobs, they need training. And we will do that using concrete little pills to help them solve new problems. And that is what we call the "five-star Constellation". And for now, we will not talk about knowledge. We will gradually fold that into the narrative, right?" OK, Cristina, right.

Hephaestus used that narrative to introduce the Constellation and geared it to the need for new knowledge to do higher value-added tasks. Agents understood that need by themselves; there was no need to push it through. And as we saw previously with I-CAN, you do not get results if people do not discover needs by themselves. Getting it right means getting every agent to see clearly how any methodological approach helps them personally.[4]

Cristina ran into another conflict when working with the Emergency Unit. While spotting the benchmarks, she found some had a very high knowledge level. She wondered whether that was really necessary, and it led her to ask the one in charge if that was really the way to go. She guessed maybe not and, therefore, she wanted to run that guess by the one taking such decisions: the head of the Emergency Unit.

By analyzing each case, it was found that responses varied from job to job. It was necessary in some, not in others. So as not to waste resources, Hephaestus decided that spotting the level of knowledge needed for doing each job was indispensable. Knowing more than necessary was not productive,[5] since acquiring more knowledge had no reason to enhance efficiency. Starting with the five knowledge levels already mentioned in Chap. 3, Hephaestus spotted tasks, knowledge and levels. In order to find today's benchmark as well as being able to tackle tomorrow's tasks.

When all this work had been done in Hephaestus's departments, Cristina was ready to introduce the organization to Constellation. At first, it was introduced department by department, so it would be the object of individual discussion in each department, and conclusions drawn. Next, it was introduced to and discussed with the board of directors.

As an example of the work done, Fig. 6.2 shows the Constellation in Hephaestus's Emergency Department. Let us analyze Fig. 6.2 in detail to understand what Cristina now uses as another management tool in her job.

---

[4] Excuse me if I repeat myself, but this book's motto—getting it right—is a win-win approach. Nothing gets done without this approach.

[5] The saying has it that knowledge takes up no room, but I think it does. Suitable knowledge is needed to solve problems found on the job. Some overlap might be value added when drawing up creative questionnaires. But there is definitely no need for level 5 knowledge of everything. That is really overdoing things.

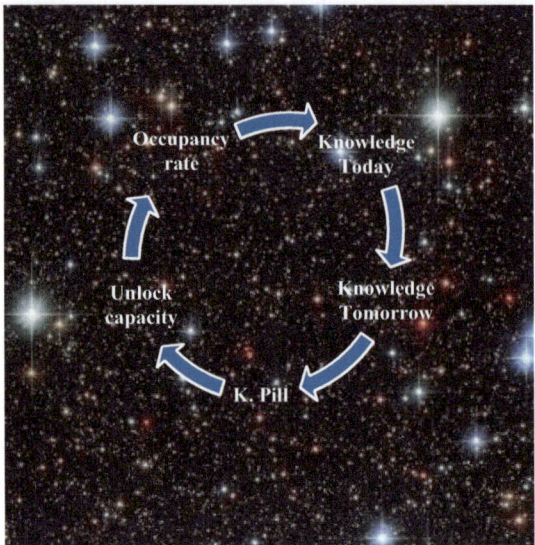

Fig. 6.2 The Constellation virtuous circle. (Source: NASA 2017)

The following text box describes the basic knowledge additions needed to perform primary tasks. Points 1, 2 and 3 identify the three department areas: head, Emergency coordinators and Verification/measurement technician.

Key to Knowledge in Hephaestus Emergencies

1. **Head of Emergency Unit**
   Knowledge of Emergency Plan NT-500
   Basic knowledge of gas distribution, installations
   Knowledge of the Hephaestus grid
2. **Emergency shift coordinators M (56%) L (5%) N (52%)**
   Technical knowledge emergency service response
   Current rulebook applied to emergencies
   Knowledge of the Hephaestus grid
3. **Verification/measurement technician**
   Knowledge of verification/measurement rulebook
   Interpreting verification certificates
   Technical and field knowledge of an installation's elements

In Fig. 6.3, we see circles (our stars) with a number inside. That number is for each person's occupancy rate in Emergencies.

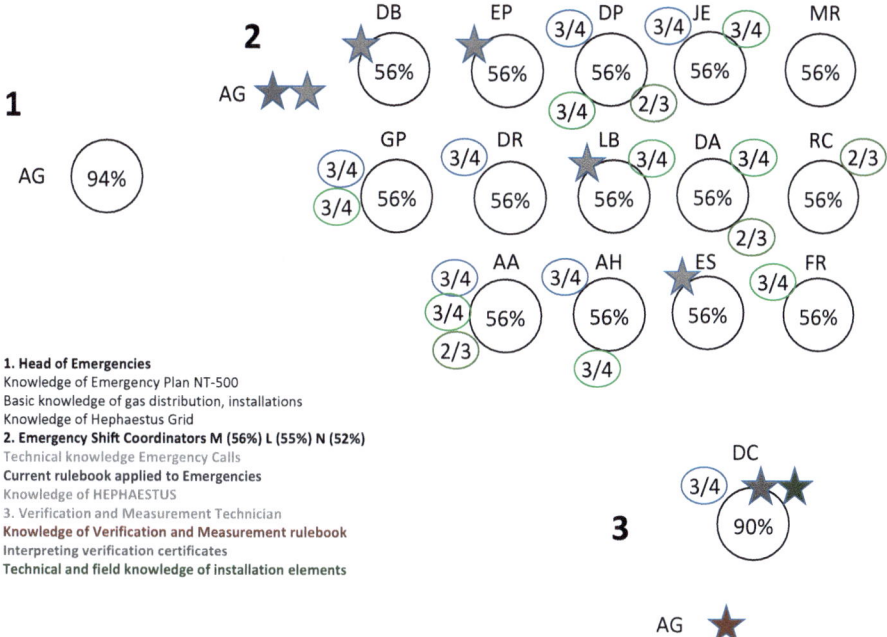

Fig. 6.3 Five-star Constellation at Hephaestus Emergencies

1. *Head of Emergencies*. The overall head of Emergencies (AG) has an LTA[6] occupancy rate of 94%. As we have seen in Chap. 3, acting to compress time he spent on interruptions is quite consistent with unlocking capacity. Service problems are constant at the present occupancy rate. Now look at AG, he has three differently shaded stars. At Hephaestus, they have spotted high knowledge-level stars. Therefore, AG is the group's wise man. He knows most about the current rulebook applied to emergencies, the Hephaestus grid, and the verification and measuring rulebook.

2. *Emergency coordinators*. In group 2, we see there are more people with a star and that means they are benchmarks in the clusters of star-intensive jobs. The three coordinators have an occupancy rate of 56%, the target suggested by the Grid Operations director,[7] a board member in charge of the Emergency Unit. Beside each agent we see some little ellipses with numbers like 3/4 or 2/3. The first number (3) shows the knowledge level they have, and the second (4) the level they should have. Thus, AA has level 3 technical knowledge and should have level 4. Meanwhile, the same AA should

---

[6] Long-term average.

[7] Remember Chap. 3.

have level 3 knowledge of the Hephaestus grid although he has level 2. This outline reveals the knowledge gaps. Hephaestus devised its training plan by following the gaps in each of the company's departments. The plan focused on filling said knowledge gaps spawned by needs inherent in solving today's problems. In addition, along with the area heads, Cristina analyzed what knowledge needs would be most critical for tackling tomorrow's problems.

3. *Verification technician.* A specialist that should keep acquiring knowledge, although they already know most about their field. This group also includes the head of the Emergency Unit (AG) as the rulebook wise man.

The Constellation in Other Companies

Achilles had also been imbued with Constellation and entrusted the capacity analysis to the Organization & IT department, and the knowledge analysis to the HR department.[8] Hephaestus as well as Achilles decided to link tasks to problems, and then to knowledge. Unbundling tasks hindered them. Culling knowledge at this level of unbundling was enough to achieve targets.

From day one, Achilles linked its transformation plan to its knowledge plan. For them, it was absolutely indispensable to spot the knowledge required for the new perimeters they were to broach. As we have seen, this link was somewhat more forced at Hephaestus. The Emergency Unit saw it clearly because they urgently needed to learn about the new secondary activities they had to tackle. In other areas, their interest was directly proportional to the challenges posed by new activities. In those that steadfastly industrialized and had to tackle new activities, they bought into it right away. For others, the path is proving to be more fraught.

This is food for thought. Should knowledge be forced through? Sincerely, I think not. The area itself must find out how the problem = knowledge binomial helps it to be more efficient. For that, starting off with a capacity analysis is indispensable. Tackling capacities, efficiency and industrialization naturally leads to unlocking capacity. And the question that always crops up is, what for? When it is understood that it is for new tasks, it is bought easily, with no fuss.

---

[8] How to split up the Constellation is a very particular issue for each company and its operations culture. There are no rules for it. The aim is greater agility and efficiency; it is for the board to decide how to apportion responsibility for each of the Constellation's components.

Artemis saw no need to act explicitly on knowledge stock. They did understand the importance of training to get across a message tied to the essence. They drafted Family members into their training courses to put across the essence's concepts. They also worked on materializing knowledge in manuals, and spotting positive experiences in the chain to join them up.

But neither directors nor head office deemed it important to bother spotting current knowledge gaps or future needs to meet changing demand. I think that was a blockage, not to combine this job with an in-depth study of new client archetypes that could approach the hotels. Part of the Family's— and most of the managers'—idea was that the client types would not change. Thinking only of demographic types, and not understanding future clients' anthropological and sociological components, may be dangerous. Obviously, suffice to say that with a business-as-usual scenario in the ecosystem, the knowledge they already possessed did not need much renewal. A strategic approach could query that scenario, as the hotel business is one of the sectors with the greatest revolution looming.[9] Strategy, archetypes and knowledge are intimately linked.

Knowledge Pills and Implementation Distance

A blocking factor that may surface in implementing Constellation is the training plan. Training has always been understood as an essential SPDM tool and training plans as the ideal way to develop knowledge.

However, once it was implemented, we met with a snag. At times, plans are drawn up in an office, with a suitable conceptual approach, but without concisely legitimizing their aim. "Why do I have to learn that?" an agent asks. This question is far more common than often thought. It is thus essential to see training as a practical KISS tool, linked to a target. This is the Constellation narrative: "You don't have that knowledge, and must have it to solve these new problems you will face." Period. Obviously there can be no beating about the bush. The approach must be straightforward, simple and swift. And this is where the knowledge pill concept arises: a knowledge tablet to solve a particular activity problem.

---

[9] Like it or not, change is currently embedded in our workaday world. Companies are undergoing big and small changes, and being unprepared can be the death of them. And some sectors are feeling it more than others. The hotel business among them.

We do not intend to dismantle your companies' training plans. They must carry on. We merely wish to stress that Constellation pinpoints the knowledge that will be needed; a swift way to get it must be designed.

And here were run into another problem: people do not read. Every day, more and more, we get back to the oral tradition by using YouTube.[10] Such conditioning requires rethinking how to convey knowledge in pill form. It has already been done at Achilles. YouTube pills that garner straightforward and concrete lessons. Who makes them? Well each task's benchmark does. Simple, cheap and quick. Moreover, it sends everybody a very important engaging message. The one that performs tasks optimally must teach the rest. We all learn from each other.

Achilles' TREASURE project, combined with I-CAN, is doing just that. And the results thus far have been spectacular. The trainees' learning curve has steepened three times, on average. Meaning that people learn in a third of the time. Moreover, they can check as much as they like as the pill is readily available. In addition, pills have industrialized the educational process and compressed time taken to teach departmental staff, since YouTube clips are very effective. Interruptions have been reduced, as pills become a source of information and checking how to do the job.

Achilles itself was surprised at the effect produced and has begun a little inquiry to gather data on just how effective the pills were. They are therefore analyzing the compression in time[11] taken in direct training, and looking at the impact on the current learning curve versus the TREASURE curve using three components: time taken by experts in training, start-up time in doing the first job, and compressing time taken by experts to answer queries.

Pitching pills and the focus on training has been welcomed warmly at Achilles in the light of prior events. At first the transformation plan was coupled with a training plan. They had begun to implement this training plan, but with very poor results. People did not understand why they needed training in other tasks, or what the reason for it was. Time consumed in training was very high and was seen as an almost pointless exercise. After G12 got

---

[10] Let us seek alternative learning formats to those established in the last century. Reading is a luxury for some, not for others. In my opinion, it depends greatly on upbringing and what you have seen at home while growing up. But even so, innate behavior and genetics come into play here. Let us accept that and seek other ways to convey knowledge.

[11] They will measure:

1. Consumption cuts like speed in performing a task, by merely considering the time to complete the task, while keeping up quality (reliability in service delivery). Benchmark—best time in the team.
2. Cuts in repetition. Number of times a task needs to be repeated to meet the target time, compared directly to the time taken by a fully trained person.

going and the transformation changed course, it was seen clearly that the training focus was not very efficient. It was disruptive and causing a lot of needless internal buzz. The training process was halted, its need reassessed and it was rejigged to provide the knowledge required by specific agents to perform new tasks. By joining the latter to the TREASURE project approach, and pills, the resultant Copernican shift calmed the waters and focused everybody's efforts.

The conceptual basis for the disruption caused at Achilles is simple and based on the implementation distance. When agents face a new task, they most often have a knowledge gap. Depending on the problem and the variety of knowledge needed to solve it, that gap has either a simpler or more complex composition. The length of the path taken to fill that gap, and give agents the knowledge to tackle the problem, is "the implementation distance".

Agents must be clear about the challenge they face, what they know about meeting it and what they do not know. And fill in what they do not know. But if we remove the "what for" aim from this equation, we return to the lack of clear purpose situation.[12] The first component in making things happen is having a totally sharp focus and purpose. The second is spotting the knowledge needed to meet the challenge. And the third is acquiring that knowledge with the aim of sorting out the situation.

It must be understood that I am talking about the business world, not the academic or educational world. That is quite different. In the business world, results are needed in the short, medium and long terms. An R&D department usually thinks in the medium and long terms. But even so, knowledge gaps are filled in with a clear aim: to find a new product, develop a new molecule or design a new fashion range. With a clear focus. Companies are about getting results to make them sustainable and adding value to society. For all those reasons, implementation distance is closely linked to the focus on effort and challenges.

Depending on how complicated the gap is, it may be filled in with pills or need a more comprehensive transmission. Learning to solve a problem that has already been solved, materialized and industrialized is not the same as solving an exploratory problem. That is why the distance is measured.

Using its Constellation approach, Hephaestus designed a training plan perfectly suited to its gaps. They did so following standard procedure, but kept the sense of simplicity and focus. Artemis produced a totally conventional training plan with just one difference, as we have said that it introduced transmitting the essence. Artemis pondered transmitting new on-site procedure

---

[12] Yes, I repeat myself. But we have seen that it keeps cropping up.

manuals using pills to be learned using iPads. Constellation may be coupled with technology to streamline and individualize learning. Each brain works at its own speed, and pills are adapted to each individual.

Knowledge Planning and Rolling Forecasts

Planning and rolling forecasts are tools in everyday use in a factory. If physical goods must be produced, nobody doubts plans must be drawn up to organize the machines' capacities. And that initial planning may undergo changes because the product sells more or less than expected. And that is where rolling forecasts come in. Client orders tend to change and consequently so must manufacturing, and when orders peak, then machines will work overtime and a second production shift start up. It all makes sense and manufacturing then responds to commercial demand.

And what happens when we produce services? Can we plan? And what do we plan?

Yes, we can plan. Moreover, we must plan.[13] Plan what? Obviously, for the flow of clients or services we must produce. Pegasus set up a weekly planning and rolling forecasts committee. The committee watchdog was the Operations director. It was attended by all areas involved in making sales happen. It was typical of Pegasus, where the Himalaya syndrome was deeply entrenched, that it was hard to get things moving. As ever, brainpower did not enter open hostilities but waged guerrilla warfare instead. Group components which turned up without preparing tasks, without following up agreements, failed to show up, and so on. Sounds familiar? Yes, it's brainpower's typical response when they have no choice but to pretend to participate, yet do not want to. How to fix that? "It's like this," the Operations director said, "Either you show up and make the plans and required adjustments, or things will not be made to happen. Any request made outside this committee does not exist." This director's middle name is Perseverance and he did not let up until the participants began to see that it was really useful to meet once a week, and analyze market behavior and needs. I will not hide the fact that the CEO scheduled the meetings in his diary and, after his first unannounced appearance, said he would attend whenever his schedule allowed. Meaning? That committee has come to stay and is so important that the head honcho attends now and again.[14]

---

[13] We cannot commit ourselves 100% to demand. Demand can be engaged with in many ways.

[14] We must never underestimate measures like this. CEOs are very persuasive. They must be asked for help. Obviously, that means they will be included in proposals made, and understand how important the whole approach is in making things happen.

But there is another type of planning: planning the knowledge stock we shall need to cover the new services we shall deliver. Or the stock we shall need to meet more demand, because we have a very high occupancy rate that will lead to backlogs. That is the new approach to planning that few companies adopt. Achilles did so. It was obviously needed, because capacity in some areas was unlocked that would have to be handed to others. And to do that, spotting whether existing knowledge stock enabled tackling new needs was vital.

HR management was very much the leading player in the knowledge issue. The manager worked side by side with G12 to use every prototype and development as a source for feeding knowledge profiles. G12 decided a monthly meeting needed setting up at board level, wholly devoted to knowledge planning and rolling forecasts. And the CEO should steer that committee.

With the CEO's agreement, regular Wednesday board meetings at once became knowledge/services planning and rolling forecast meetings. First requirement specified: the need to know in time the knowledge profiles required to meet new demand. Determine whether new incoming issues were to tackle already-known problems or new perimeters that needed new knowledge stocks. The committee has flourished after several meetings held to adapt.[15] Knowledge needs for the next six months have been spotted and they have decided who to give those tasks to.

HR is already aware of needs and closely working with the outcome of I-CAN and TREASURE. The leg that needs most effort is spotting individual occupancy rates. A group-by-group estimate has been made, but individual calculations are needed to correctly assign planning requirements. To this must be added the need to implement the CSI new services project, which requires matching agents' occupancy rates to the required knowledge stock.

Many Achilles directors' operations dream is to have all the suitable information needed to offer a service "at their fingertips, anywhere in the world".[16] Their wish is to spot each agent's occupancy rate and knowledge. In so doing, they could estimate at first glance whether a request suddenly made to them could be quickly accepted or not. That is the aim of Constellation at Achilles and they are hard at work on it. The following text box sums up the seven points in Constellation's whole structure:

---

[15] Human beings clearly shun planning. It is hard to commit to the future. It is much easier to live by fits and starts. But fits and starts are very harmful to knowledge. Fits and starts lead to suddenly hiring people without developing in-house people. Remember: NO HIRE, NO FIRE.

[16] As they belong to a multinational company, their constant globe-trotting means they need their information as accessible as possible.

The Five-Star Constellation

1. An individual capacity analysis to spot:

   (a) Primary and secondary tasks
   (b) Occupancy rate in primaries
   (c) Benchmark of who does the jobs in the least time

2. Diagnosis of each agent's knowledge level for performing tasks at present
3. An assessment of each agent's knowledge level for each of said tasks
4. Knowledge planning and rolling forecasts in the company's operating strategy
5. Spotting new tasks to be tackled and knowledge needed, as well as each one's knowledge level
6. Spotting individual knowledge gaps for each agent's new tasks
7. Planning to devise knowledge pills to obtain new knowledge stock

Knowledge Units

Pegasus figured it had no need to act on the knowledge "leg" in its Constellation. Its knowledge stock was not the problem; it had enough and did not foresee big structural changes on a ten-year horizon. Its initial focus was time compression. Getting there demanded that Pegasus do away with bottlenecks, and therefore they performed capacity analyses. Likewise they set up a Rapid Intervention[17] unit to back up different areas that needed to analyze bottlenecks and diagnose occupancy.

Pegasus did need to implement another SPDM idea: Knowledge Units (KUs). Remember that a KU is a club where agents share experiences in developing knowledge, solve exploratory problems and grow around issues they are keen on. The KUs support the Business Units (BUs) to solve problems so fraught they need a high knowledge level. It gives Achilles' wise men stability. Pegasus needed to drive horizontal knowledge cores, and for that they devised two KU prototypes: Everest and FACTS. Each KU had a coordinator in the Processes area to steer its creation methodologically, and follow it up.

Everest KU

Everest is the name given to software written "Himalaya style" by Pricing, but was used by much of Pegasus and the extended enterprise. Using it caused many headaches, because only a few knew how to solve the problems Everest caused. Many questions went through official channels, but many others

---

[17] The Processes Department, reporting to Operations, has a small group trained to that end.

Everest KU Rulebook

I. *Aim*

- To set up a multidisciplinary expert consulting group to deal with and fix problems relating to Everest or its operational functions, to serve as a baseline and touchpoint for the whole organization. Organization is understood in its broadest sense, under the extended enterprise umbrella.

II. *Functions*

- Concentrating formal and informal knowledge, using reactive or proactive measures, to share with the rest of the Organization
- Develop exploratory measures, seek to solve problems that have not been considered beforehand or require research to be solved
- Support for industrializing the service
- Materialize knowledge stock
- Support for spotting or defining developments in Everest

III. *Scope*
Within *scope*: solving unstructured (exploratory) problems related to Everest and its operational functions. Those problems' causes may be:

- New problems arising or known problems whose solution is unknown, or if known, there is a problem when implementing it
- Previously solved problems that arise, but the rest cannot solve
- Recurring queries due to lack of familiarity with the software, or relating to the business's operations
- Recurring incidents
- Indications and guidelines (if needed) on how to solve an applicative problem
- Support for spotting or defining developments in Everest due to solving problems posed

Outside *scope*:

- BAU mode consultations
- Functions covered by a functional unit
- Occasional incidents due to the software

IV. *Roles*

- Group leader (watchdog). Shall ensure the unit's smooth running and steer the solving process in case some barrier or discrepancy exists. The leader must have enough autoritas.
- Solving process's sponsor. Shall be in charge of seeking the solution to the issue or problem posed. Naming the sponsor will depend on the types of knowledge required.
- Rest of members must be advised of the issues and problems assigned to the unit. They may play a part in solving processes to support the sponsor.

V. *Solving process at the Everest KU*

Once the *Everest* KU leader is named, the latter shall name a sponsor to take charge of seeking solutions to the problem posed.

The sponsor must:

- Analyze it and confirm the type of solving process to apply; applicative or exploratory. (N.B. a problem may be applicative or exploratory depending on a person's knowledge).
- Estimate a due date for fixing, according to impact and need.
- Propose a joint solution with other members or functional units chosen. This process must consider possible alternatives for implementing the solution, and must always be coordinated with the functional unit in charge of implementation.
- Advise Processes of the proposed solution.
- Record the solution in the knowledge database, in VOC format.

VI. *Follow-up and industrialization*

Once the solution is proposed, Processes shall:

- Advise those affected.
- If needs be, coordinate with the functional head over starting to implement the solution and who must ensure correct implementation.
- Industrialize the solution (standardize it, where applicable).

The Everest KU must assess, based on solving problems, whether the service needs redesigning or some action plan needs carrying out.

VII. *Operations rules*

- There are no hierarchies. There are no bosses in the KU, only experts.
- It is not a functional business unit (BU). The BUs provide service problems and the KU is there to develop knowledge to solve them.
- Pending, definition of prioritizing criteria for KU members intervening vs the user's own workload.

stayed in limbo, as nobody dealt with answering them. It was thought that setting up an Everest KU could sort that out. The KU would take charge of those questions to answer them in a reasonable time. That would benefit Pegasus as well as the extended enterprise.

The Everest KU's duties were devised under Processes (see following text box). "Members shall represent various Pegasus functional units and need not be high level. Members shall have level 4-5 (expert) required knowledge. As for the extended enterprise, each one shall have a contact person, so they shall be specialists and contact persons for issues to be dealt with or implemented. They shall not be part of the KU to begin with." The extended enterprise would have to take part in the KU once the KU was consolidated in Pegasus. This would be of great benefit as it would allow direct input into the KU of problems close to end customers, and add new knowledge blood and problems when implementing Everest.

The way to proceed is sketched out in Fig. 6.4. A user has an Everest problem. As Everest is a software development, the first to come across the problem is the Systems area. If it is within their sphere of knowledge, they solve it. If it is not within the software development sphere, Systems hands it to Processes, a department under Operations. Processes sees whether the problem is entered in the knowledge database (KDB) in verb, object, condition (VOC) format. If the problem is recorded (applicative) or there's a similar one, the user is advised.[18] If it is new, it is handed to the Everest KU. They tackle/solve the problem and hand the solution to Processes. Processes tells the user and industrializes the solution.

Pegasus has not incorporated that KU into the extended enterprise and that step is pending. The more feedback there is from implementing in the extended enterprise, the more the knowledge developed for the KDB.

Currently, the KU has stalled a little as the handing of Everest development has been transferred completely to Systems. Users are focusing their problems on workaday operations issues and new problems are not arising that require the KU's support. The KU is reassessing its contribution and seeing how to channel its knowledge stock to support exploratory problem-solving in the Pegasus sphere.

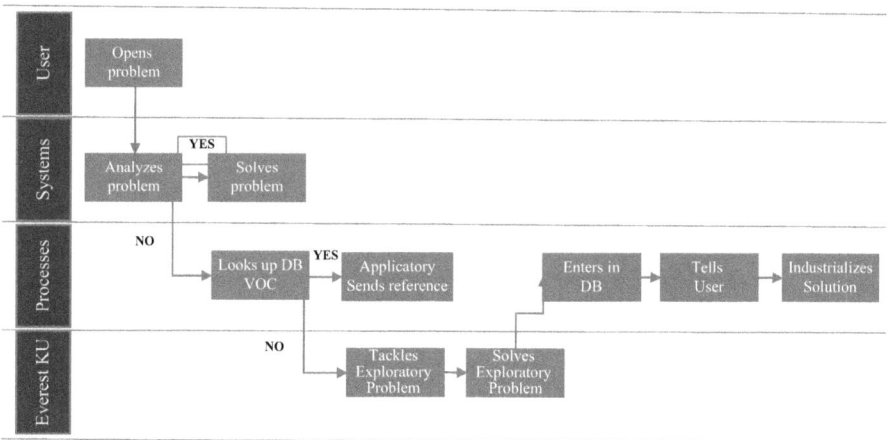

Fig. 6.4 Flow of Everest and Everest KU problems

---

[18] Readers may wonder whether it would not be easier for the user to look at the database directly. This is effectively the case if the user fully understands the problem's cause. If they do not, they need support from Systems and Processes to spot possible solutions.

FACTS KU

FACTS is the second KU. Its aim is to set up action guidelines to be followed in managing and controlling data at Pegasus. For that they need to rely on Pegasus people that have high-level knowledge of data management problems. The KU's methodological structure is based on Everest and replicating it (following text box).

FACTS KU Regulations

I. *Aim*

- Create a multidisciplinary expert consulting group to implement and maintain the Pegasus data model.

II. *Functions*

- Data Government Model
- Support implementing said model throughout the organization.
- Receive and channel departmental feedback on Data Government that may help to modify and adjust the model.
- Concentrate formal and informal knowledge about the information in Pegasus.

III. *Scope*
Within scope:

- Indications and guidelines (if needed) on how to solve an information problem affecting several departments
- Receive and channel departmental feedback on Data Government that may help to modify and adjust the model; entry channel for modifying the model.
- Support for spotting improvements or issues for completion or inclusion

Outside scope:

- Occasional incidents affecting only one function or department

IV. *Roles*

- Group leader (watchdog). Shall ensure the unit's smooth running and steer the solving process in case some barrier or discrepancy exists. The leader must have enough autoritas.
- The solution's sponsor. Shall be in charge of seeking the solution to the issue or problem posed. Naming the sponsor will depend on the types of knowledge required.
- Rest of members must be advised of the issues and problems assigned to the unit. They may play a part in solving processes to support the sponsor.

V. *Operations* rules:

- There are no hierarchies. There are no bosses in the KU, only experts.
- It is not a functional business unit (BU). The BUs provide service problems and the KU is there to develop knowledge to solve them.

As it is a somewhat particular KU, since it is not composed of those that know most about data as such, but those that know most about problems entailed in bad data, its head wanted to greatly enable communication between its members. Therefore, relations between members will be constant and informal, with no need for sophisticated technology. They communicate by email; they have a KDB in VOC format for internal management and have set up shared folders.

At present, the FACTS KU is operational, focused and getting results in formalizing the model. It holds meetings every month, approximately. It promotes improving consistency in data used by Pegasus, cutting costs in managing it, and their greater and better availability in supporting the decision-making process and meeting information needs. Every Pegasus department takes part.

Both KUs are deemed prototypes to learn from before implementing new KUs at Pegasus. Implementing them has demanded effort from their heads, as well as crucial support from Processes. The path becomes simpler once the methodology and experience are there.

The KUs are a help to Constellation. When the Achilles CSI spoke of its wise men's committee, or "area 20", it was pitching the embryo of a KU. Constellation is the individual response to each particular agent's need to acquire knowledge. The KU is there to make available knowledge for the whole organization to solve the most fraught or exploratory problems. Both measures may be combined, since they tackle different situations. And they are perfectly symbiotic.

SPDM Concepts Used in This Chapter

Chapters referred to: 6, 7 and 13

In this chapter, we introduced new SPDM concepts, the five-star Constellation and brought back the knowledge pills introduced in Chap. 2.

Knowledge pills are knowledge materialized and focused on supporting the way to solve a particular problem. They are a new way to transmit knowledge to speed up learning. Given that adults do not read, the idea is to make pills in YouTube video format to use as a visual aid for transmitting the knowledge required to solve a particular problem.

Since knowledge levels were reviewed back in Chap. 2, and capacity analyses in Chap. 3, the next SPDM concept to stress is implementation distance. It begins by classifying innovations spawned by the problems that must be solved. We have defined two categories of problems: structured and unstructured (Chap. 5). Each has two properties in turn: low or high variability (Table 6.1).

Table 6.1 Problem types (Muñoz-Seca 2017)

Structured	Those that may be solved by applying a sequence of operations, or problem-solving process. Solutions to such problems will come with an applicable solution process
Unstructured	Those for which, *a priori*, it is impossible to find what solutions are satisfactory. Solutions to such problems will come with an exploratory solution process
Low variety	The problem may tackle one area. Implementing the idea may shake up a small area
High variety	The problem may tackle several areas as a whole. Implementing the idea may shake up a large area

These four components have a mix that creates four types of innovation shown in Table 6.2. Implementation distance measures the knowledge gaps available to tackle each type (point I in the Conceptual Appendix). The greater the distance, the more difficult it is to see realities and the more preventive work that needs to be done on knowledge stock.

Implementation distance is tied to planning knowledge stock. If planning exists, rolling forecasts exist. A rolling forecast (RF) is empirical proof that what was forecast is real. It is the adjustment needed. Problem demand undergoes alterations, and thus the problems that come with knowledge available to solve them must be adjusted. And that is an RF's function.

The other important SPDM concept is the Knowledge Unit. A KU is a club of people that meets to solve novel problems and support the Organization. There is no revenue expected here. They are there to provide solutions that the rest of the organization, with a lower knowledge level, cannot. Or would take much longer to find.

Conceptual indications given to Pegasus for setting up KUs were as follows:

Table 6.2 Innovation types (Muñoz-Seca 2017)

Incremental	Tackles structured and low-variety problems. Problems where solving changes is at local level and entails a small change
By extension	Tackles structured and high-variety problems. Problems whose solution will have an impact on different units; although the changes will not be big, they will require several departments to coordinate them
Radical	Tackles unstructured low-variety problems. Problems whose solution will be at local level but of great impact
Revolutionary	Tackles unstructured and high-variety problems. Problems whose solution will have a great impact on the whole company and that require much coordination between the various units

Structure of a KU (Muñoz-Seca 2017)

The idea is simple. It is about imitating a club's social structure. Citizens in society belong to clubs or associations where they find an atmosphere suitable for their physical, intellectual or professional development. Clubs offer their members activities, led by an organizing committee in charge of the club's activities. Citizens may belong to as many clubs as they please, and such activity overlays their own economic activity. They may leave messages and hold virtual meetings, which does not imply coordinating schedules and minimizes time-wasting. The idea is that every employee in the company belong to the necessary clubs so they have adequate support for their development. These clubs will be mostly virtual, that is, they will not demand meetings to do their job. Technology has given us the chance to do group work without needing the group to exist physically, as such.

Moreover, the KU develops the capacity of its members to use that knowledge in their BU operations. The KU is not responsible for the outcome of applying that knowledge. That outcome is linked to customer service and is thus the responsibility of the BUs, not the KUs.

- Starting with the KDB, group knowledge types for setting up Knowledge Units.

  - Choose as many as you wish according to the knowledge found, and add more or less knowledge.

- Knowledge bearers will be KU members.

  - They can, and must, have different knowledge levels. Spot them.

- A KU's aim is to develop the assigned knowledge.
- KUs are dynamic and may be modified as needs be.

  - They must not be shackled to company functional or departmental units.

- They may be constituted by staff from the company, and companies participating in the extended enterprise scheme.
- They are not responsible for the outcome of applying said knowledge.
- Each KU must have a watchdog.
- KU heads must consider the following issues when it comes to developing their components' capacity:

  - How problems are solved in the KU.
  - How to improve the way to spawn ideas.
  - How to find alternatives for using the KU's knowledge in the BUs.
  - What blocking factors prevent implementing new ideas?

- What prevents thinking outside the box (what barriers exist)?
- What tools we would need to develop our way of thinking.

The following text box shows the methodological way of setting up a KU, and there are some tables to help out in the appendix (point II in the Conceptual Appendix):

Way to Set up a KU (Muñoz-Seca 2017)

1. *Spotting KUs*
   We can get the company's KUs by diagnosing knowledge. People bearing that knowledge must belong to the KU; they are its members. That structure means a person may belong to a diverse group of KUs depending on their knowledge profile. A KU's virtual and many-sided nature makes such multiple membership feasible, with no complications.

2. *Spotting KU components*
   For that, the bearers of expertise need to be spotted. This task is simple and usually overlaps with the previous phase. Everybody in the company must be assigned to one KU, at least. Otherwise, we have found somebody that adds no knowledge to the company. That situation is a sign that the knowledge inventory process has been superficial or incomplete. It is worth rethinking the analysis to track down the anomaly.

3. *Documenting relations between KU components*
   Now the KU must be given an internal structure. There are no bosses in the KU, only experts. And as it is a structure based on authority, it is easier to constitute that structure around natural, existing (and probably accepted) relations between KU members. The role that each bearer plays must be spotted, and for that the people that facilitate solving others' problems must be spotted, the ones deemed more creative by other participants and that they go to when implementing ideas.

4. *Spotting critical people in the KU*
   The critical people are those that support the greatest number of relations. At least one of them must play the role of KU watchdog. The watchdog's leading role is the KU's handling and working to improve knowledge contained in the expertise that defines it. The watchdog is the catalyst for improving and must have a very proactive role.

5. *KU tasks*
   The *KU's* aim is to develop the capacity of its components to apply existing knowledge in improving the BUs represented in that KU. Thus each KU participant's aim is to find ways to apply knowledge to improving the BU they belong to.

Chapter 6: Conceptual Appendix

I. Innovation matrix

P **R** Un **O** Structured **B** **L** **E** Structured **M**			

Low variety	High variety

II. Knowledge Units

List of Knowledge Units	
Date KU established	KU startup date

Knowledge Unit X	
Date KU established	Watchdog
Participants	

7

Problem-Solving Tracks and Service Modules

Abstract This chapter shows how to focus brainpower on an efficient problem-solving approach. A track is a highway for specific types of service problems in which particular agents, who have the knowledge required to tackle those problems, solve them. It is articulate because it allows agents to skip from one highway to another, depending on demand. Tracks run through service modules. Any service is composed of a set of service modules that can either be located inside the company or the extended enterprise ecosystem. Service modularity makes for high flexibility. The chapter shows how one company has implemented both tracks and service modules.

What Is a Track?

Some years ago I did a job for a law firm. There I found empirically that there was room for many basic operations ideas in the 100%-services world. And there the tracks concept was born. A track is a freeway, a fast and perfectly enclosed highway along which a certain type of problem can move efficiently.

A service is a set of problems that must be solved. Some of these problems are perfectly defined; they recur and may be perfectly industrialized. Others are more complex and require creative input in order to be solved. The level of creative input is determined by how complex the problems are. Some need to combine simple knowledge types to fix the situation. Others, larger-scale knowledge types to fix another situation.

© The Author(s) 2019
B. Muñoz-Seca, *How to Get Things Right*, IESE Business Collection,
https://doi.org/10.1007/978-3-030-14088-5_7

Each company chooses how to define the problem type driving along the freeway, depending on its individual circumstances. Often the incoming volume on freeways determines how each freeway is defined. Therefore, determining what may drive along each freeway depends very much on a company's situation at a given time. And it is flexible depending on how the company wishes to organize it. Such flexibility is one of the great advantages of tracks, as it makes for speed and streamlining.

Let us look at a couple of real examples of freeways.

One way to distinguish between them may be the complexity of the problem per se, without bearing specific issues in mind. In this case, one freeway may focus on simpler problems and another on more complicated ones. Thus, one freeway may be solely earmarked for processing claims over different banks' minimum interest rate clauses (simple) and another for processing claims by holders of preferred stock in particular companies in the Basque Country (complex).

Another option is having the freeway focus on particular issues, for example, divorces, but with two lanes along which different-colored cars may drive depending on the extent of the problem. Lane 1 for simple divorces (yellow, divorces by mutual agreement) and lane 2 for complex divorces (green, divorces with custody problems and many assets). The yellow cars will drive much faster than the green ones. The yellow cars will be much more industrialized and automated than the green ones. They all drive along the same freeway, some at 100 mph, others at 55 mph, depending on how complicated each case is.

Regardless of how the freeway is defined, each car has a driver to drive it to its destination. The number of drivers needed depends on how many cars will be driving. More on some days, less on others. The freeway is made of rubber to adapt to the flow it absorbs, and will widen or narrow down, depending on the number of cars it needs to egress. The input of cases determines how wide the freeway is.

The so-called dispatchers handle incoming cases. Cases may come in previously classified by freeway. Or it may be the dispatchers that classify them. That depends on each firm, the volume received and the level of industrialization that the case classification may have. And on the knowledge profile the dispatchers need. In the case of law firms, a dispatcher was somebody with horizontal knowledge of what was coming in, and was capable of classifying input.

After reviewing the input, dispatchers analyzed demand and assigned cases to drivers. And they assigned cases depending on each driver's knowledge stock. Freeways accept cars and drivers depending on the knowledge stock needed to drive on them.

For example, let us look at the case of the "preferred" freeway. It is Friday today and dispatchers analyze the input received to plan for next week's "preferred" freeway. After analyzing the estimated consumption the cases will require, they decide that 25 drivers will be needed next week. They assign 25 drivers from the pool to the preferred freeway for next week. The pool is the Constellation where each driver's knowledge and availability is defined. Which is to say that drivers in the pool are identified by the type of car they can drive, and whether they are available. Drivers may drive along several freeways, as they have the knowledge stock to do so. Dispatchers optimize the resource by assigning drivers to the freeways they deem most suitable. This means dispatchers, if they do the classification, must know the Promise's priorities and expected response times for each client archetype. Thus they make their forecasts by estimating the required response time for each service on each freeway.

A problem may arise when dispatchers do not have enough drivers. This possible lack of capacity means forecasts must be made at least quarterly. Planning and rolling forecasts, and knowledge stock, are the tools for making such forecasts. Knowledge stock is not obtained overnight. Therefore, there must always be buffer knowledge stock. Such buffer stock does not lead to inefficiency, as an agent may be using other knowledge types on other jobs, but there is a buffer in case demand peaks. Thus drivers must be partial-knowledge multitaskers available for different tracks. Given that drivers can drive two or three cars along different freeways, the knowledge mix they have balances out one freeway that they drive along with another.

Another situation that may arise is that one driver may be a specialist and only able to focus on one freeway. This undermines flexibility, but may be necessary to offer very complex responses. The solution is to give such drivers specialty primary tasks, but also plan to assign them specialty secondaries that may add differential value. In law firms, for example, those specialists devised modules that were then used on other tracks to industrialize tasks. Devising models is a secondary task that may be planned for and, nonetheless, adds much value to the group (Fig. 7.1).[1]

The beauty of tracks is that drivers change freeways and set constant challenges for each one. Such planning is very changeable and spurs development of the drivers' knowledge. Different problems spawn learning. Moreover, tasks that become repetitive may be automated, thus unlocking capacity so that drivers may go faster, or along shorter distances.

---

[1] Remember that secondary does not mean it has no added value. Secondary is synonymous with plannable. In a brokerage, for example, company or sector research is indispensable when advising clients. But they are secondary tasks performed during a broker's downtime. A broker's primary task is placing and selling securities.

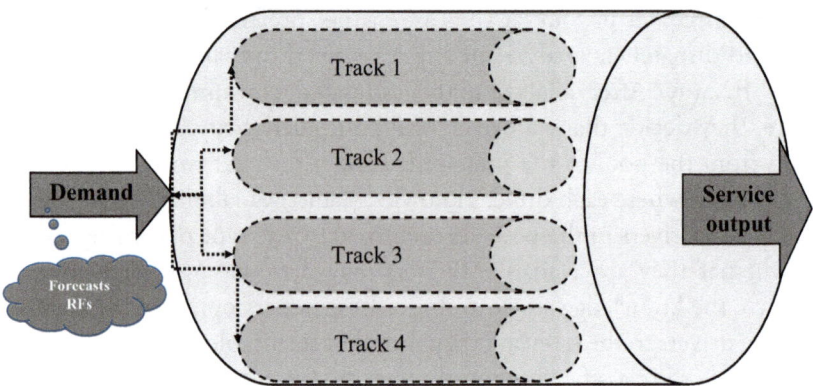

Fig. 7.1 Tracks

As previously mentioned, perfectly implementing tracks requires the five-star Constellation approach. Each driver must be clear on what they know, and what they do not but should know, in order to tackle future demand on freeways other than the ones they are assigned to. Likewise, each driver's occupancy rate must be known, depending on their knowledge of each freeway and availability.[2] And if new freeways are to be built, the new resources needed must be planned for so they will have drivers. All changeable, adaptable and streamlined.

Our Companies and Tracks

As readers will appreciate, so far we have been dealing with theory in an ideal world. Practice is a far cry from that. For now, none of the four companies featured in this book has such tracks perfectly in place. Achilles is nearest to going along such a path, as it is using the tracks concept in several of its areas, but so far as a prototype concept. Achilles is indeed working on Constellation, where implementing tracks is the obvious way forward.

Pegasus has "handmade" its adaptation to tracks in its Pricing area. It is a small group of 20 people. The two heads of both areas know their people perfectly well, and have spotted their knowledge and their gaps. They have not gone about Constellation in an academically acceptable way, but they do have their own approach. As seen previously, they did a capacity analysis[3] to

---

[2] This is a constant we have seen throughout this book and I shall not repeat myself.

[3] This they have done in keeping with suitable academic guidelines and the SPDM way of operating. But of course they didn't do so, that was the Processes Intervention group's doing!

find their group load, but did not do so individually. And at the overall company level, they are the bottleneck that prevents Pegasus getting the response times it needs.

To tackle said bottleneck, they began to carry out all the efficiency measures described under different headings in previous chapters. Once those measures were implemented, and finding the times were still not as required, the area had to be rejigged. To do that, one of the ideas they used was an ad hoc version of tracks.

They defined five tracks depending on the type of case or measure they came across. One of the tracks was earmarked solely for performing audits and information tasks required by a higher body. This body made requests at a particular time of year, and that made the area totally collapse. In line with basic planning principles, a very high percentage of tasks were spread out among the 12 months of the year. And likewise, a corresponding forecast was made to spot when demand would peak, to have capacity available for tackling incoming jobs.

Planning was especially important for the other four tracks. Two complementary measures were spotted: the need to boost capacity and redesign the specified Pricing process. Both options were tackled in a different way.

Capacity was boosted by devising a track for a specific type of problem, which was assigned to an outside company that performed the tasks while following guidelines set by Pricing.

Redesigning the process came about using automation and industrialization. A track was devised with the help of automation to compress time and simplify matters. In the other two tracks, and depending on each one's particularities, tasks in general have been modeled to industrialize operations and there has been a second round of simplifying operations.

Tracks have helped people with greater knowledge to perform higher value added tasks, by unlocking capacity from lower value tasks. The latter have been rationalized/automated or assigned to outsourced tracks. This job is beginning to bear fruit and time has been compressed considerably. When that job is done, the bottleneck will move on to some other part of Pegasus.[4]

Hephaestus applied tracks in an interesting way. Part of the Expansion area was focused totally on converting to gas. The targets set by the CEO were very aggressive and the department was overwhelmed, or so they said. The outcome was that, indeed, the targets were being met, but countless administrative loose ends were left, which then greatly hindered daily operations with new clients.

---

[4] Remember, bottlenecks do not go away; they just move on.

The "sweepers" track was devised to fix that problem. Its name says it all. Sweeping up after the hordes have passed. That track was earmarked for tying up loose ends after the conversion. It was not a permanent track, but had been set up to fix a particular situation at a particular time. The track was not meant to be solidified, as the area ought to have tied up operations perfectly, but when they found that impossible in practice, they decided to establish the track.

I do not advocate establishing one in every company, but I have observed in many that some cases were halted because of some missing document or clarification. And those halts may become neglect. Setting up a sweepers' track to clean up what has been halted, due to lack of information or updating, may help to streamline response times and compress them. Once the incident has been fixed, the case may return to its natural track to run its course. That worked at Hephaestus, where they have since dismantled it because it is no longer needed. A temporary solution to a temporary problem. It is most important such solutions do not solidify.

Tracks are, therefore, a response to the need for flexibility and streamlining that a company needs nowadays. Their elasticity allows them to stick to clients' needs and rationalize demand. It all revolves around the knowledge stock the drivers have. Thinking that drivers can be total multitaskers is utopian and very expensive. But partial multitasking that allows them to drive along a couple of tracks is indeed very convenient. That smooths out peaks/troughs in demand and rationalizes agents' needs for solutions. Drivers are constantly challenged, as being on different tracks makes them grow. A dispatcher sets the tone based on demand and fulfilling the Promise. The rules of the game are clear to everybody, and everything is driven by the capacity to solve service problems. Growing means delving into new tracks. It is win-win for the company and drivers.

Tracks will not tolerate inefficiency and duplication. They demand a lean structure where each driver focuses on their tasks by doing them in the simplest way possible. Technology supports them and frees drivers from tasks that add no value for them. New services may mean new tracks or new lanes on the freeway. It all depends on need and the knowledge requirements that the service demands. The Achilles CSI is studying that makeup, because new services on the horizon, possibly, will require somewhat extensive internal changes. For all those reasons, an ideal tracks activity requires eliminating wastefulness, *muda*,[5] and for that, service modules must be implemented. Let us see what they are and how they are implemented.

---

[5] Remember, wastefulness in Japanese.

Service Modules

In the course of its time compression work, Pegasus found much inefficiency and duplication. That duplication affected not only the company itself, but the extended enterprise, too. Pegasus needed streamlining. A first efficiency round got good results, but another step forward was needed. The current service settings were not suitable and needed to focus on designing a service that would afford it greater flexibility. Issues undertaken in the company today had to be handed to the extended enterprise, and issues in the latter had to be performed, for efficiency's sake, inside the company. Exchanges and joint design had to be built up for Pegasus, as well as what would be handed to the extended enterprise.

The service model they were after had to have clearly defined and identifiable components, like Lego bricks. And also to be able to decide, according to company timing, whether Pegasus should execute the components immediately, or hand them to the extended enterprise. That modular idea, very common in software companies or in the aerospace sector, where everything is done by modules, had to be adaptable to a 100%-services-based financial firm. To get there, Pegasus decided to implement the operational design settings using service modules. So as not to argue with other areas, as the word "services" seemed to send messages the organization was interfering,[6] Pegasus began calling them operating modules, given that the Operations area would handle resetting the service design.[7]

A module is a box. Where problems go in and solutions come out. Input and output. The boxes make up the different groups of activities in the promised service. And they may be in the company or the extended enterprise. A modular unit provides streamlining to obtain the optimal combination of modules both in the company and in the extended enterprise. Pegasus adopted the following definition of operating module: "A set of tasks developed by people constituting an indivisible operating unit under a sole head. Such minimal management units allow services to be implemented—both internally and externally—as the operating modules deliver their results to other modules. The operating modules likewise work independently of their organizational location."

---

[6] When the concept was understood fully and the Operations Settings area proven to be a help, the modules were given their proper name, that is, service modules.

[7] I think it is obvious but want to stress that such a step requires approval from the CEO and managing committee. Changing to modules is an important step, as the operational design is reset. It requires full backing from senior management. Without that backing, such a transformation cannot be considered.

Each module has one or several clients. Each one specifies the features of the service required. And expects to get the service according to said specifications. The module promises to deliver the client the service according to those specifications. Therefore, each module must translate said specifications into operational settings that allow them to be fulfilled.

Each module has one or several suppliers that hand it elements so the module can assemble the service it provides. The module, in turn, specifies each element it needs from its suppliers. It is a continuous chain of specifications. Just as a module may have several clients, it may also have several suppliers.

Pegasus said; "We want to be able to plug and unplug modules in the extended enterprise whenever convenient, so we can tackle time compression and operational streamlining."

For its part. Achilles is studying the feasibility of implementing service modules when building a service offering, in the CSI project. Breaking down a service into modules would allow it to add and take away components, depending on clients' requests, thus cutting design time in building a service.

The Operations Settings area, reporting to the Pegasus Operations management, took the reins in the work to modularize the company. The organizational structure was left alone. Already-existing departments were merely modularized. To enhance clarity and the aim of the new operations functioning design, Operations Settings defined its support functions when creating modules (following text box), and shared them throughout the organization.[8]

Pegasus Operations Settings Functions Regarding Operating Modules

- Set up necessary operating modules.
- Locate operating modules.
- Set up the operating module:
  - Necessary inputs
  - Operations rules
  - Outputs for management control and supervision
  - Outputs for different sectors
  - Scalability guarantee
- Plan the load for each module so that it can give service to different services that require it.
- Define load analyses to comply with planning and specifications.
- Implement KPIs and SLAs to measure each module's efficiency and efficacy.

---

[8] Many ghosts are seen and companies full of brainpower see things everywhere. Balloons must be burst constantly, and facts and realities exposed. And prototyping must be done. Prototyping does away with smokescreens and exposes realities. Never forget, with brainpower FACTS; FACTS; FACTS.

The Settings area wanted very transparent actions. They needed other departments not to feel wary, but support the modules. For that they did some internal marketing and showed the need to set up the modules. The targets given to the whole organization for the operating modules were:

1. Simplify operations:

   - Eliminate duplication.
   - Eliminate unnecessary approval levels.
   - Delegate tasks that add no value to defined targets.

2. Boost efficiency:

   - Segmenting processes to seek optimal management
   - Industrializing
   - Measuring by indicators and service levels

3. Making actions more autonomous:

   - Manage operations by defining guidelines.
   - Guarantee results using KPIs.
   - Supervise using people in charge with an executive view.

4. Boost flexibility and adaptation:

   - Cigar store model any manager can manage
   - Adaptable to possible changes in manager or setting
   - Response to modifications and quick transition

Pegasus's idiosyncrasy made it essential to draw up operating rules, without which everybody would take on the modules every which way. The modular approach requires uniformity, as the client provider chain demands it. The rules drawn up were:

- Each operating module shall have a single person in charge of operational settings and supervising execution.
- An operating module shall be understood to be autonomous/self-contained and indivisible when it comes to implementing business lines and initiatives.
- An operating module may be reused in different services in different business lines.
- Operating modules may be added together to define a service.
- Operating module does not mean outsourcing. Pegasus shall decide when it is time to outsource an operating module, or not, but its settings, supervision and execution will be run regardless of the decision to outsource.

Components in a Module's Settings

Internally, a module (Fig. 7.2) has its operational settings designed using three sets of SPDM elements:

1. The six variables that define the operating structure and its settings, according to the service Promise
2. An internal and external *Indicators structure* relating to clients/suppliers: SLAs and KPIs
3. The knowledge stock

   1. The six variables approach (processes, capacities, flows, HR profile, information systems and operations rules) provides the basic operations design. Depending on what each module promises their client, that is how its settings will be structured. For example, a same-day response time with variable demand will have a capacity setting with low occupancy rate for primaries, in order to be able to adapt to fluctuations. If demand is known and planned for, on the other hand, occupancy rates may be higher. Industrialization and automation must be tackled when designing settings.[9]
   2. Modules' customer and supplier relations are managed by SLAs. A module's internal functioning is monitored using KPIs directly related to the SLAs the module has with both clients and suppliers. It is recommendable

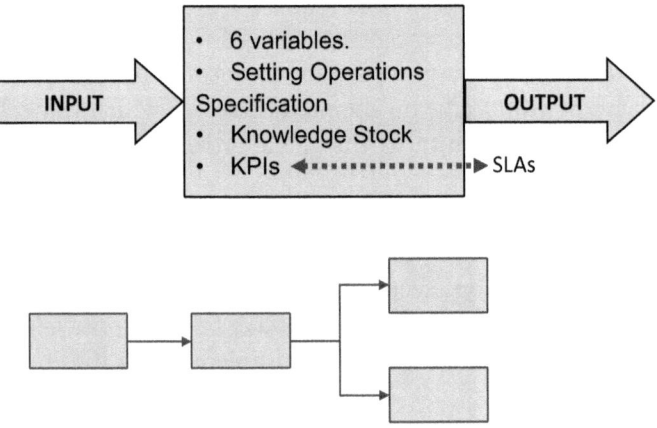

Fig. 7.2 A service module's components

---

[9] If the automation business case does not turn out to be suitable, at least spot what F5 tasks currently exist in the module, so as to be able to act on them and unlock capacity second time round.

LEVEL	KNOWLEDGE
[1]	Financial.
[2]	Bankruptcy.
[1]	Risk Analysis.
[2]	Handling Internal tools.
[2]	Office automation.

Fig. 7.3 Aggregate knowledge in a back office module

not to set up more than two or three KPIs and/or SLAs in each module. An example of a KPI is, "Total number of cases sent back as a proportion of total cases received," or "Average time taken (in days) between sending back a case and the extended enterprise submitting it again".

3. Another fundamental component is the knowledge stock of the agents assigned to the module. The knowledge required to perform the module's tasks, and a suitable level thereof, must be found. Having Constellation helps greatly and makes the task easier. As an example of knowledge stock, Fig. 7.3 shows the knowledge types (added together and at the required level) for a Pegasus back office module that we shall analyze next.

Prototype in the Service of Case Management at Pegasus's Back Office

Following the SPDM approach of always prototyping before large-scale implementation, Pegasus began modularizing with the back office (BO). The BO is a service that Operations offers the rest of Pegasus. The BO would become a prototype for learning how to implement modules, and was meant as a baseline for showing contributions to efficiency and streamlining. The fact the BO had a very large extended enterprise component likewise favored its choice. Every goal has been reached and the BO prototyping has been a total success. The most troublesome client was Pricing, so next we shall describe part of how the work done was developed.

As a first step, the service modules were broken down. The BO's Case Management service with Pricing as client was broken down into nine operating modules.

1. *Escalation quality.* Check documentation and information for escalating documents to prevent future returns in analysis and Pricing processes.
2. *Templates.* Obtain abbreviated data that clients require from each document.
3. *Following up returns/incidents.* Check for diligent management of returns due to the need for more information on the deal.
4. *Following up formalizations.* Check for correct reporting of formalizations.
5. *Following up future commitments.* Check for correct application of future commitments in formalizations.
6. *Closure.* Check final status of cases.
7. *Clearing up documentation.* Adapting documentation provided to documentary standards, to allow more efficient access.
8. *Documentary completeness.* Find and recover documentation missing from cases depending on their closure.
9. *Commissions payment control.* Guarantee payment of commissions arising from sales, corresponds to correctly managed deals.

In a first phase, they spotted seven elements in each module:

1. Who is the client?
2. Who is in charge of the module's output?
3. What factor caused its production?
4. What is its raw material or input?
5. What is its deliverable or output?
6. KPIs.
7. Knowledge stock and possible task automation.

Table 7.1 cross-references the BO modules with the seven elements described.

Table 7.2 shows an example of two BO module's features: Escalation quality and Templates.

In a second round of prototyping, another element was added: the head of production. This official makes sure that planning and rolling forecast needs are suitable for correctly executing the module's output.

Making clients understand the importance of planning is no mean feat. Bad planning alters the service's realities or makes the structure idle. In the case of Pricing, the first demand figures produced were much inflated, which consequently led to inefficiency because the structure was idle. Almost all the BO's processors worked in the extended enterprise, but even so, as capacity

Table 7.1 The BO's Case Management service modules and their components

	MODULES								
	Escalation quality	Templates	Following up returns/ incidents	Following up formalizations	Following up future commitments	Closure	Clearing up documents	Documentary completeness	Commissions payment control
Who is the client?									
Who is in charge of the module's output?									
What factor produced it?									
What is its raw material or input?									
What is its deliverable or output?									
KPIs									
Knowledge stock and possible task automation									

Table 7.2 Escalation quality and Case Management templates modules and their specifications

	Escalation quality	Templates
Client/s	Pricing	Pricing
Head of production	BO	BO
Production driver	Monthly organization	% Monthly organization
Basic input	Proposals to escalate	Proposals to escalate
Basic output	Escalation OK Escalation blockage	Standardized data
KPI	1. In/out 2. Pending stock 3. % Blockage/cause 4. Process time	1. In/out 2. Pending stock 3. % Returns 4. Process time
Knowledge stock	1	3
Automation	80.00%	80.00%

was hired on a monthly basis, forecasts wide of the mark led to underutilization. And losing money.

Installing the head of production was no mean feat. Firstly, the ideal person had to be spotted. And to do that a detailed description of the module was needed. That allowed roles and workloads within the module to be found. To convince other modules that the head's role was important, pilot heads were found that would be benchmarks within Pegasus, so as to prove their roles were efficient.

The importance of planning and rolling forecasts had become so evident throughout Pegasus that, in some services, ad hoc Production forecast modules were set up. This model's focus is planning workload. Likewise, to bring about mutual learning, periodic meetings have been scheduled to follow up and drive the production bosses' role. These two measures recall the I-CAN methodological drivers at Achilles.

It took four months to establish every service module in the BO's Case Management unit. The modules were implemented in order. Once the project had been wholly implemented and up and running for three months, the head of service and the Operations Settings coordinators thought over the blockages that had been found, and what could be learned from them to use when implementing the next modules. They thought over what might be learned, as did those in charge of I-CAN at Achilles. Thinking over that way focuses on spotting the blockages in operations culture that may arise when introducing SPDM innovations.

The Pegasus project group summed up its thoughts on learning, from introducing the service modules scheme, under four headings: overall project definition, client's role, module settings and execution.

1. *Overall definition of the service modules project*:

   (a) Not detailing FTE from other areas (heads or clients) delays development. To this must be added the difficulty in spotting new roles introduced by service modules.

   (b) The project's road map had been managed by temporary interests not always shared by other areas involved.

   (c) Applying methodology to concrete problems produced quick deliverables, but reduced overall understanding of the project.

2. *Client's role*:

   (a) Spot the client:

      a.i. Many possible clients and must be formalized.

      a.ii. Nobody feels they own it: Negotiate level of responsibility and, by default, the head of project's imperatives.

      a.iii. No room for function in any current company area: ask HR department.

   (b) In a model like Pegasus's, clients may be outside the extended enterprise and we need direct outside access.

   (c) Clients neither take on nor exercise their role

      c.i. Does not follow up

      c.ii. Requests things other than those agreed, without foreseeing impact

      c.iii. Does not complain about breaches

   (d) In every case mitigation entailed using the head of Production as a mover, and holding project follow-up meetings.

3. *Module settings*:

   (a) Modules will work out easily if procedures and instructions are previously defined in the traditional way (procedures, etc.). If the module's need is spotted but guidelines are pending, it inherits the complexity of defining a new procedure.

   (b) Due to lack of data and history, defining the production forecast will be hypothetical. This hinders capacity analysis, as no time ratios are available.

4. *Execution*:

   (a) Difficult access to outside executors, even in the extended enterprise
   (b) No feedback into planning in line with developments
   (c) Mismatches in dimensioning and thus breaches in SLAs signed due to the aforesaid

Those four headings clearly show how modularization is synonymous with new rules of the game, new roles and new obligations. They do not touch the organizational structure, but they do set up a new way to take on responsibilities. And that is obviously somewhat unsettling. With modules up and running, many can no longer hide nor hide inefficiency. They lay bare many actions and show up wastage, duplication and inefficiency.

Joining Tracks, Service Modules and Knowledge Units

To sum up, we have seen thus far:

- A track is a freeway for problems along which cars (service problems that need solving) are driven by agents that possess the knowledge stock required to be located on that freeway.
- A module is an indivisible unit that receives an input and delivers an output, and has clients and suppliers. A service is a bundle of modules.

What is the relationship between tracks and modules? Figure 7.4 describes this. A track may go through one module only, or several. The freeway may be concentrated on only one module's geography (like an island), or pass through several geographies (as in an archipelago). Tracks spread between several modules because their knowledge requires more than one module. One knowledge type may solve a group of problems. These problems may be unbundled among several modules. The aim is always to simplify and streamline, so intermodular tracks are more flexible and better withstand demand swings.

A module in turn may have one track or several, depending on the types of problem flowing through it. Remember it is dispatchers that assign drivers/cars to tracks. At times some tracks may perfectly happen to be empty. Or they may vanish from a dispatcher's job because they have been automated and solve problems themselves automatically, 24/7.

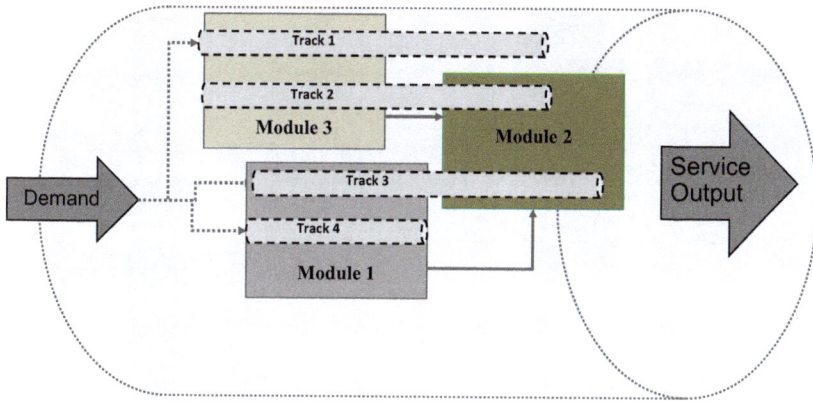

Fig. 7.4 Joining tracks and modules

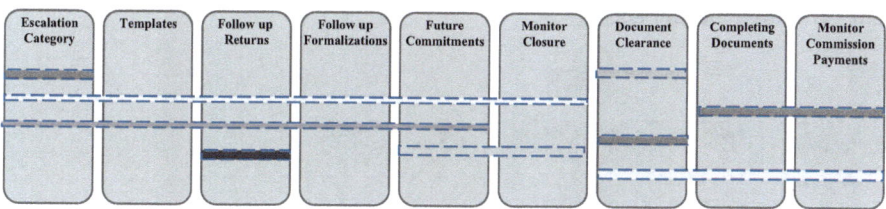

Fig. 7.5 Joining tracks and modules in the BO Case Management unit at Pegasus

Figure 7.5 shows BO Administration's nine service modules and possible tracks to set up. Pegasus right now is looking into how to structure inter-modular tracks, because it designed only intramodular ones in the first phase.

An interesting observation is the ease with which those modules were handed directly to the extended enterprise (unplugging Pegasus and plugging in the latter) or vice-versa. BO execution at Pegasus has now been completely handed over to the extended enterprise. Specifications, planning and the head of Production were all defined within Pegasus. The service was produced by a third party that received a perfectly specified order and a detailed follow-up, using KPIs in place for complying with said specification.

Pegasus could decide, anytime it suits the Operations Settings, that some of the BO modules become internal, and leave the extended enterprise with another section of modules (Fig. 7.6). Clients will see the whole service and their touchpoints will be whichever ones Pegasus decided on as critical times for fulfilling the Promise. Pegasus could likewise demand that the extended enterprise add a head of production to receive periodically the necessary indications. The flexibility for action is total. And the streamlining immense. The

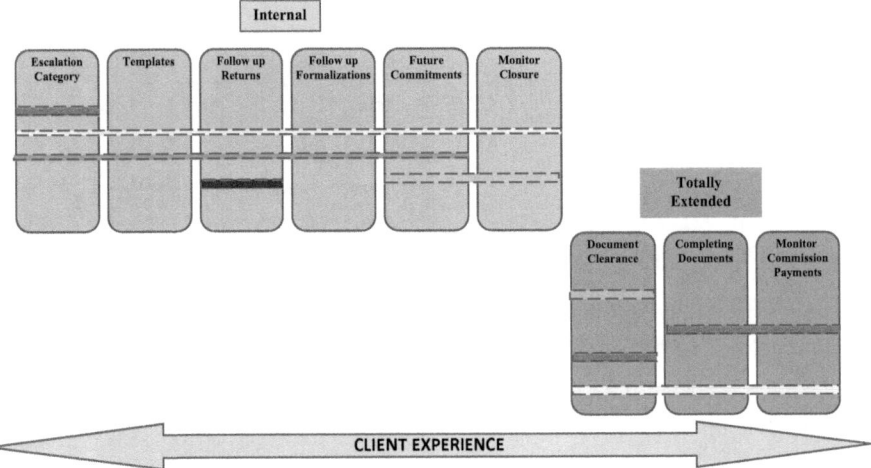

Fig. 7.6 Internal modules and modules in the extended enterprise relying on the client's end-to-end experience

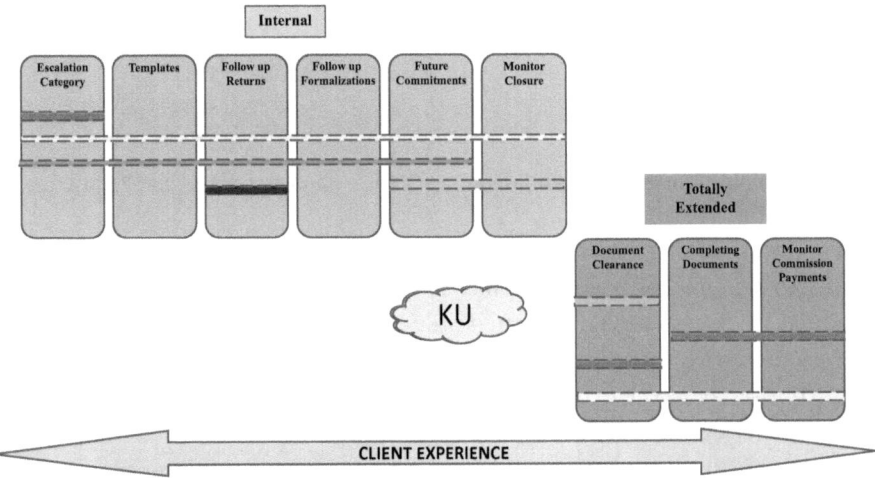

Fig. 7.7 Internal and extended enterprise service modules and knowledge units

only demand is to have a specialized service and possess the knowledge stock suited to timely follow-up of the KPIs that will enable understanding the causes of possible breaches or difficulties.

Another service modularization scenario involves finding when the extended enterprise has more knowledge than the company outsourcing execution. In that situation, the company must define the specifications and elements for following up as exactly as possible, and let the extended enterprise function as a "black box" in providing the service as promised.

In any of the two scenarios, it adds much value to establish Knowledge Units that complement modularization (Fig. 7.7, example for Case Management at Pegasus). Those KUs will be composed of members of the company and the extended enterprise. Each with different knowledge levels of the subject matter emplaced. Thus the KU becomes a knowledge broker[10] handing out complex evidence and situations to both players, the company itself and the extended enterprise. Solutions to new problems will be found in the KU, and each player will add their knowledge stock to solve them. They are the ideal setting to share and create new solutions, since they add complementary views of problems.

SPDM Concepts Used in This Chapter

Chapter referred to: 10

The chapter as such develops the SPDM concepts sketched out in my previous book. The tracks and service modules have been developed afterward due to the need that has arisen upon implementing SPDM ideas in the companies. They are thus new SPDM conceptual material.

The modules' settings do follow the six operations variables in the previously published SPDM model. Therefore, I wish to stress how such an analysis must be performed (point I in the Conceptual Appendix). The settings come with the four standard ways to compete: price, specialty, innovation and flexibility. Depending on each module's priority service criterion, its variables will adopt ad hoc settings to provide the service output. If the module's demand is very random, its settings will be closer to flexibility. If, on the other hand, demand is stable and planned, its settings will tend more toward cost. It is up to each module's watchdog to decide on the service settings, depending on the specification agreed with the client (Fig. 7.8).

The following steps must be taken to conceptualize the operational settings:

A. Define each variable as an extreme value for fulfilling the module's Promise:

  – Each Promise requires different settings for its variables, which in turn will give us a specific competition model for each company.

---

[10] Broker: person that, by trade, acts as intermediary in deals to buy and sell exchange-listed shares and financial securities.

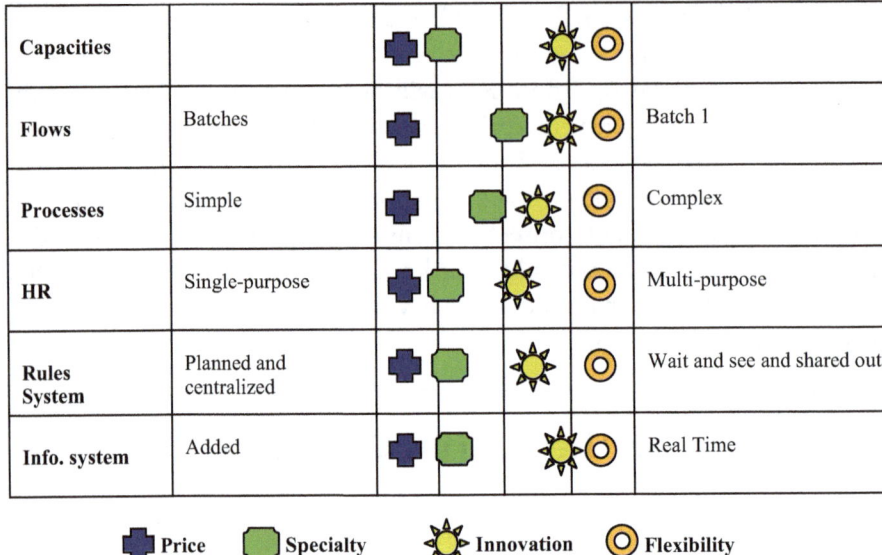

Capacities				
Flows	Batches			Batch 1
Processes	Simple			Complex
HR	Single-purpose			Multi-purpose
Rules System	Planned and centralized			Wait and see and shared out
Info. system	Added			Real Time

Price   Specialty   Innovation   Flexibility

Fig. 7.8 The six variables' settings according to the way to compete

- – Give each variable two extreme values to ease our positioning in one or the other.
- – Use logic to relate the various variables.
- • If cost is a priority dimension, the agents' occupancy rate will be high.
- • If response time and product range are priorities, occupancy should not be high as agents must adapt to constant change.
- • Very high-percentage—or indeed low-percentage—capacity may be used.
- • Clients may be handled in large batches or batches of one; we may also think in terms of process solutions, or sequential goods, or simultaneous goods.
- • Processes may be either simple, or more complicated and sophisticated.
- • The HR profile may be single- or multipurpose.
- • The rules system may be centralized and planned, or indeed spread around depending on developments.
- • Decisions added to the information system (IS) every so often or in real time.

B. Think about your dimensions and priority criteria.
C. Define your ideal profile for fulfilling the service promise made to the module's client.

Chapter 7: Conceptual Appendix

Variables' values (situate the module)				
Planned, high occupancy				Subordinated, low occupancy
Batches				JIT, batch 1
Simple				Complex
Single-purpose				Multi-purpose
Expected and centralized				Wait-and-see and shared out
Added				Real time

8

Altogether Now! We Need Everybody's Effort Implementing the "9 Questions" Tool

Abstract Win-win is the key approach in order to achieve results. This chapter addresses how our four companies have faced the win-win challenge with the help of the "9 questions" tool. This tool offers the basis for implementing SPDM operational culture. It provides nine concrete questions that any manager can offer his team, in order to destroy any blocking factors that the team might encounter, so as to achieve sustainable efficiency.

The operations culture that goes with SPDM is about mutual gain, for those involved as well as the company. It is critical that each implementation measure is a win-win situation for both.

A very effective tool for making this operations culture happen is "The nine questions". Remember briefly[1] that those questions analyze the three primordial mainstays in SPDM operations culture:

- Efficiency in agents' performance (Efficiency)
- Individual and organizational learning (Attractiveness)
- Getting all agents on board the way to operate (Engagement)

Each mainstay may be broken down into three questions:

1. Efficiency: What must be done? Who have I assigned? Who is in charge?
2. Attractiveness: What service do we provide? What must I do without being told? Who helps me grow?

---

[1] See Chapter 14 in my *book How to Make Things Happen*

© The Author(s) 2019
B. Muñoz-Seca, *How to Get Things Right*, IESE Business Collection,
https://doi.org/10.1007/978-3-030-14088-5_8

3. Engagement: What are our targets? What are our values? What management style is needed?

The nine questions have two particularly important uses. One is the *Board of Directors' guide*. It is used to spot existing operational malfunctions and build consensus among members. Without clarification or consensus among Board members, the company will not proceed at the right pace and a great deal of energy is wasted on wholly pointless matters.[2]

The second use for the nine questions is in an *interdepartmental session* with the aim of getting embedded problems in the Organization to surface. Those elements are grouped together to make up projects, in order to smash the blockages that prevent reaching the targets required to fulfill the Promise. The session must start with the CEO spelling out the Promise, essence and flame red. Once clarified, the nine questions will gently focus the interdepartmental session's thinking to spot blockages that prevent the Promise from happening.

Members taking part in the session must then be members of the work groups detailed to fix existing blockages. Participating from day one allows each member to feel engaged in doing the job, to have the authority to polish up or modify problems, and to be able to speak up confidently as the project is developed. Everybody has their role, and just as work groups hold no sway in defining or assessing the Promise, they do hold total sway in spotting blockages that exist in the company, in order to make things happen. Not spotting those real difficulties along the way is one of the great pitfalls in making things happen. That explains the chapter's title. If we do not act altogether now, things are not made to happen.

The main focus of such an interdepartmental session must concentrate on the issues the CEO is worried about. Pegasus focused it on "*response time compression*", Artemis on "*efficiency and engaging everybody to get a differential service based on essence*", Hephaestus on "*what stops us being a 4.0 company*", and Achilles on support for thinking about the desired "*operational culture style to better engage* all participants in the 2020 Achilles Transformation Plan".

Let us look more closely at how "The nine questions" helped each of our four companies to make things happen.

Artemis

Artemis's work began with a session where every hotel manager, leading members of the central structure and part of the Family took part. Previously, the Family and CEO had held a work session to spot the Promise, essence and Flame Red in order to use those concepts in the interdisciplinary work to be done.

---

[2] Power struggles are pointless as far as I am concerned. I know others do not think so, but I do. A waste of time based on egos. Whenever I can, and they let me, I shoot them down. Personally, I have no time for mediocrity.

Management and the Family shared with the group the priorities entailed in the Promise,[3] essence and flame red. Next, in small groups, the participants spotted blockages in making the Promise happen. The problems were jointly unveiled, since making every group member take an active part puts in place an operational culture of trust and transparency.

Once the blockages were spotted that prevented the Promise from happening, those same groups then spotted what blockages existed in Artemis in order to answer the nine questions properly. Once again they were contrasted at group level, agreed on and listed.

Blockages preventing the Promise from happening were listed, as well as blockages that hindered answering the nine questions. Every participant assessed the joint list, according to the priorities the Family and CEO had given to the Promise's dimensions.

Once filtered, there was a list of 64 elements. The ten blockages that had the greatest impact on making the Promise happen and answering the nine questions are shown in Table 8.1.

Once those ten blockages have been analyzed together, and based on others that contributed value added to those ten, the group settled on seven projects to be worked on for seven months. Those projects were as follows:

1. Decision-making
2. Updating workstation knowledge + skills
3. Organizational structure
4. F&B: client experience
5. Reset operations: service design
6. Methodology for efficiency
7. Client archetypes

The implementation distance[4] was assessed for each project to spot the existing knowledge gaps that prevented making the projects happen (Table 8.2). According to the participants in the work session, there would not be too much trouble in implementing projects 5 and 7, and 1 and 4, since they focused on known (structured) problems.

Events have corrected that initial appraisal. For workload reasons, the CEO decided to postpone the archetypes project and steer it in another direction afterwards. Artemis, like every company in its sector,[5] is in the throes of a

---

[3] See Chap. 1.

[4] Remember Chap. 6.

[5] In July 2018, Spain's National Statistics Institute (INE) tallied 28.5 million overnight stays by foreign tourists, 2.2% down on the same month in 2017. The trend is downward and that means redesigning the service or sliding into a price war. Big mistake!

Table 8.1 Highest-value blockages according to impact on Promise/nine questions at Artemis

	Overall service margin	Agility in making decisions	New ideas for daily services. Creativity	Service provision	Reliability	Sum Total
Promise assessment	1	1	2	4	2	10
Blocking factor						
1. Fear of change, skepticism	2	5	8	16	8	39
2. Need to update the playing field, infrastructures and attitude	3	2	6	20	8	39
3. Means–infrastructures	4	2	10	16	6	38
4. Slow decision-making if the answer must come from head office	2	5	8	16	6	37
5. Above-average F&B	4	4	6	16	6	36
6. Blockages in experiences and feelings	2	4	6	16	8	36
7. Slow communications	3	1	6	20	6	36
8. We are unaware of clients' expectations	1	4	4	20	6	35
9. Lack of time and stress stop us being friendly	2	3	4	20	6	35
10. Decision-making time is blocked by a certain absence autonomy	2	5	6	16	6	35

Table 8.2 Implementation distance in Artemis's projects

Unstructured problems will arise	3	Organizational structure	2	Updating work station knowledge + skills
	6	Methodology for efficiency		
Structured problems will arise	5	Change operations settings: service design	1	Decision-making
	7	Archetypes	4	F&B: client experience
	Low-variety problems will arise		**High-variety problems will arise**	

backdrop undergoing volatile changes in clients and their habits. Understanding those changes in depth would have been a major driver in redesigning the service. The two projects were symbiotic, but when the archetypes failed, the huge impact service design would have on Artemis was blurred.

Projects 1 and 4 concentrated effectively on structured problems that could be solved operationally. Project 6 was a pleasant surprise, as the work group detailed to it absorbed the methodology perfectly and got excited over capacity analysis. As seen in other chapters, its use led to very interesting conclusions. The CEO and the Family took care of project 3. Finally, project 2—considered the most revolutionary—was another pleasant surprise as the team worked most satisfactorily on all of its contents.

Once the projects were defined, work began on implementation. For that, a project chief was named and each group's components found. Each group in turn broke down its subprojects and planned plotting a Gantt execution chart for the seven months' work. The following text box lists the projects and sub-projects setup:

Project Activities at Artemis

G1	**Decision-making/makers**
G.1.1	Preview annual investment plan simultaneously with operating budget timetable.
G.1.2	Propose structured channel where information is exchanged between operations and sales.
G.1.3	Spot common rules applicable hotel by hotel regardless of location or category.
G.1.4	Hand over procedure carried out at Dunas hotel to gather clients' needs.
G.1.5	Content/reports to circulate, to provide data commonly used in TD.
G.1.6	Coordinate with project 8 Efficiency Central Office decisions on budget timetable.
G2	**Updating knowledge: Diagnosing knowledge**
G.2.1	Standardize and unify workstation types by position for Artemis group.
G.2.2	Proposal to define knowledge units (overbooking pilot).
G.2.3	Ideal profile sought after for candidate to occupy each position.
G.2.4	Induction plan undertaken at Dunas hotel to assess feasibility in rest of hotels and assess costs.
G.2.5	Propose operations rules to translate Artemis values.
G.2.6	Review and prioritize VOC problems associated with project.
G.2.7	Produce a photo album to define Artemis dress code for nonuniformed staff.
G.2.8	Review, Top 20 moments (project 5) for baselines in hotel induction courses.
G.2.9	Benchmark hotels complete dream customer journey to spot the rest's training needs.
G3	**Organizational structure (in family and CEO's hands)**
G4	**F&B client journey**
G.4.1	Fulfill F&B customer journey by extending touchpoints provided by proprietors.
G.4.2	Add a new tab to complete customer journey with common blocking points detected.
G.4.3	Define standard that meets clients' needs

G.4.4 Detect a critical blocking factor for hotel and analyze using Ishikawa diagram.
G.4.5 Go on customer journey in competing hotel to complete analysis.
G.4.6 Add success factors according to experience with Mercurio hotel.
G.4.7 Action plan to maintain standards or steps to get there, depending on current hotel situation.
G5   Reset customer journey operations
G.5.1 Complete Excel model in customer journey format, using AS IS.
G.5.2 Work plan to modernize manuals.
G.5.3 Review and modernize manuals.
G.5.4 Review content manuals to share viewpoints and decide on model and next steps.
G.5.5 Complete customer journey according to the proprietors' input.
G.5.6 Assess cost involved in fixing blocking factors hotel by hotel.
G6   Implementing methodology: SPDM
G.6.1 Capacity matrix and head office loads.
G.6.2 Draw up standard hotel administrator job description.
G.6.3 Find hotel manager's administrative tasks and look into handing them over to administrators.
G.6.4 Plan hotel capacities analysis.
G.6.5 Draw up standard hotel manager job description.
G.6.6 Find level budgetary knowledge hotel manager must have.
G.6.7 Plan visits to competing hotels to compare touchpoints.
G7   Client persona archetypes: Ethnographic techniques (postponed)
G8   Head office efficiency: Six variables method
G.8.1 Draw flowchart for requests process to find the process AS IS.
G.8.2 Analyze IT ticketing to date and propose management of issues and current requests.
G.8.3 Communicate obligatory compliance with IT tickets as only way to manage issues.
G.8.4 Establish model for standardizing suppliers.
G.8.5 Propose track for hotel operating emergencies in the request processing flowchart.

Part of the results have been shown in other chapters in this book. The project took seven months and ended just before the hotel season began. Activities listed in the previous text box were undertaken in their entirety.

Pegasus

As mentioned previously, Pegasus had a serious problem in fulfilling its service delivery times. It decided to tackle its time compression needs using basic SPDM concepts. It thus embarked on a yearlong project.

Table 8.3 Pegasus projects

Grouping	%	No. of blockages
1. Extended enterprise	13.02	27
2. Setting targets and responsibilities	38.79	93
3.	5.97	13
4.	5.05	13
5. Simplifying processes	28.97	69
6.	3.06	7
7.	4.49	20
Ungrouped	0.64	2
Grand total	**100%**	**244**

As a first step, they held an interdepartmental session to review the situation, as did Artemis. The only difference is that, as they were so focused on time compression, they also thought about blockages that might be arising due to not understanding fully the "time" factor's components. For that they used the seven times[6] structure that would allow them to spot what time types recurred most, and the blockages that prevented redirecting them.

The exercise uncovered 244 blockages (Table 8.3), which, following the same methodology shown in Artemis's assessment of the Promise's criteria and the nine questions, were subsumed into the seven projects.

In order to uphold Pegasus's anonymity, I shall only show the three projects with the greatest specific weight. These three projects would tackle more than 80% of the blocking points spotted by the work team.

1. *Extended enterprise project.* Clearly define roles, responsibilities and guidelines for relations in the ecosystem. This initiative was basic for establishing who must do what in the operations world and what could be expected from agents outside Pegasus.
2. *Project to define targets and responsibilities.* Seek efficiency and efficacy in operational decision-making, and align the whole of Pegasus with the strategic and operational targets.
3. *Simplifying processes.* Find the value chain,[7] measure, reduce and monitor it, and act on those points causing inefficiencies, while pursuing gradual implementation of initiatives to improve our operations.

---

[6] Remember Chap. 3.

[7] We affectionately call the value chain "the *churro*" as it took up the whole wall in the room we used for a year as the project's headquarters. The churro completely staged the entire flow, from start to finish, including activities and times consumed. This photo became mythical, because people gazed at it almost in wonder at the amount of unproductive time that existed. Translator's note: A *churro* is a Spanish snack consisting of a strip of fried dough sprinkled with sugar. They are so long when made that they need cutting up before serving.

To develop work on those seven projects, six work groups were set up, each with its own chief. Choosing the group chief was based on spotting people who came from areas that were not uncovering many blockages. The idea was to look at the situation with fresh eyes, using the same "think different" approach as Achilles. Each group was multidisciplinary and worked with SPDM methodology, but on the clear understanding that it was an authentic Pegasus project, with Pegasus solutions.[8]

The Pegasus Processes area would take charge of the project's overall coordination. A managing group consisting of four people was named, all from the Pegasus Operations area.[9] Systematic support for every team was introduced with a representative from Processes to take minutes, follow up and help out wherever needed.

The teams met weekly for 11 months. Talks were held with department heads to unlock capacity for each team's components, so they could fit in the project with their daily work. The CEO made an overall appeal to the whole company to explain the project's importance, as time compression was critical in achieving the results the company needed. A 10% salary bonus[10] for every Pegasus employee was linked to the project's success.

The KISS operations culture was embedded in the project, as was total transparency, win-win, he who does knows, and the extended enterprise was engaged. The groups could subcontract measures to each other according to each one's differential knowledge. Thus, very close collaboration came about as did engagement among all the participants.

A managing project group was set up. The latter met in a room set aside specially for the project, on whose walls diagrams and project processes were displayed. Meetings taking up a whole day were held weekly for nine months. Every group traipsed through the room to report on progress, analyze ongoing improvements, unblock situations that needed it, and to get help with methodology. Once a month all the group heads met with the group manager and the project manager sent a monthly report to the CEO.

A very important issue in the project was exhaustively following up the key performance indicators (KPIs) for target times that had been fixed as a goal. Two people—one full-time, the other part-time—focused on following up in detail compliance with target times. Their hard and painstaking work was greatly enriching, as it opened up areas for research that had not been considered in the blockages. Very operational issues like current stocks, stalled cases

---

[8] Remember, brainpower all the way.

[9] Director and deputy director included.

[10] The project ended with almost all the results expected so the bonus was not paid out in full, but almost. This was a thorn in the side of the manager in charge of the project.

Table 8.4 Monthly following-up of Pegasus project activities

	Under analysis	Spotting	Maturing	Approval	Under implementation	Implemented	Total		Initiatives subcontracted to other groups	Activities subcontracted from other groups
1. Extended enterprise	4	2	1	2	0	0	9	10%	1	0
2. Targets and responsibilities	0	0	4	2	2	0	8	9%	1	0
3.	0	8	1	0	2	0	11	12%	0	0
4.	0	0	8	0	0	1	9	10%	0	2
5. Simplifying processes	0	0	11	4	1	0	16	17%	0	1
6.	0	14	0	0	2	0	16	17%	0	0
7.	4	1	3	0	1	9	18	20%	0	0
8.	0	0	0	1	0	4	5	5%	0	0
Total	8 9%	25 27%	28 30%	9 10%	8 9%	14 15%	92	100%	2	3

that impaired average times, cases halted in particular places, and much else besides, were broached thanks to those two participants' sterling efforts.

The processes group coordinated the initiatives' monthly following-up. As a member of processes was detailed to every group, the latter took minutes and followed up, which made everybody's lives much easier. Initiatives were reported in the monthly follow-up of the work groups (Table 8.4), depending on their status, from analysis (-) to implementation (++). The group director followed them up weekly with the head of each subgroup and analyzed difficulties. Likewise, the director helped unblock issues that may have seemed irrelevant but prevented the work from progressing properly.[11]

At the end of one year's work, 50% of the initiatives were implemented, 25% were readapted to other initiatives and 25% left on standby. Oddly, the Operations Settings design project[12] that the Processes Department tackled next has retrieved some of these initiatives.

---

[11] It may seem irrelevant, but in every company administrative coordination of meeting times and room location has been a blocking factor. Having somebody in each group in charge of looking for rooms was most important for I-CAN at Achilles, and exactly the same at Pegasus. At Pegasus, some groups wanted to meet outside the office in order to get some peace and quiet, and work. All this mess needs sorting out, otherwise much valuable time is wasted.

[12] Already explained in the previous chapter using service modules.

The action plan was grouped under five headings. The aim was for actions to be independent of the groups' personalities, and make them consistent as a whole.

1. *Process reengineering.* Simplifying processes by getting rid of bottlenecks and adopting redesign measures focused on enabling operations.
2. *Industrialization.* Initiatives geared to simplifying work operations mainly by cutting administrative workloads, dealing with tasks in advance, eliminating reprocesses and ordering activities.
3. *Transparency and best practice.* Set of measures geared to clarifying requirements in executing operations, while incorporating experiences that constitute an optimal baseline in their delivery.
4. *Operations settings.* Define and design how services must be executed, the infrastructure to support them and detailed specifications for their delivery.
5. *Operations culture.* Make every Pegasus department is aware of how important it is to perform tasks in the least possible time.

Each initiative is linked to a proactive follow-up to dismantle any risk of it being "left in limbo". Likewise, in an ever-changing world, the need for adaptations must be considered.

Managing follow-up demanded marking them with a situation indicator to define their status: check, force or carry on.

- *Check* initiatives already implemented while ensuring they are sustained over time and/or adapted to new situations.
- *Force* implementation of new initiatives found while taking suitable action to do so effectively.
- *Carry on/maintain* work lines already carried out using new approaches and/or execution cycles.

The time compression project was finished by the due date. A one-year project was agreed to and the project was finished by year-end. Consistency is essential in such situations given that participants had to fit their daily work in with the project, and that required great personal effort. Showing that the commitment to compress time is fulfilled is indispensable. It ensures reliability, so that every participant understands that a beginning and an end are indispensable when meeting targets.

When the project was done, activities were left in the Operations area's hands. As a finishing touch, the CEO gathered all the project members together, asked about lessons learned, and congratulated the 60 members for a job well done. The measures were implemented and time compression was achieved.

Hephaestus

The Hephaestus project was geared toward the Board of Directors. The aim was to produce a wake-up call to rethink the company's way of operating, while impacting the end customer, although the latter was reached via intermediaries. There was a desire to query the whole service design and open up horizons for Board members as well as the company's top tier.

The project was undertaken during a lull in company activity, and was of limited duration. Meetings were weekly in order to set a fast intervention pace. Existing blockages were worked on from the start to keep the promise and, in parallel, so were the difficulties entailed in the nine questions.

An issue that became important immediately was the resources' occupancy rates. Thinking of a different scenario takes time; a manager put it well when he said: "Everyday work grinds me down." By working thoroughly on this component, the need to set up Constellation was spotted. Changes proposed required knowledge profiles that had to be developed. Capacities, knowledge and a new service design meant that after three meetings, Hephaestus began to draft in its second tier. Thinking of major changes without involving them would have been plain suicide. They had to be on board from day one, to really enable spotting the key areas.

Thus, coordination between directors and their deputies was key to handing the Emergencies area secondary tasks, which the Operations area was performing. Work was done in a spirit of agreement between areas, while HR manager Cristina was critical in driving home key concepts like occupancy and use of knowledge.

The work's overall tone was one of rapid intervention to get short-term results. The CEO drove all of his team to query matters, and his poignant questions made them constantly rethink Hephaestus' service elements. We might say clearly that Hephaestus underwent a small conceptual revolution for four months.

The measures that arose had an implementation distance with a longer-time horizon than that agreed on for the process's duration. Some would be disruptive, as they would change their members' working conditions. Those measures remained under study, in order to analyze the impact they would have and spot the right time to implement them.

Table 8.5 The Hephaestus Board of Directors' nine questions

	What must be done?	*Who have I assigned?*	*Who is in charge?*
Efficiency	Everyday work grinds me down	No feedback when responsibility not taken	Lack of operational decision-making
	Domino effect to convey plans	Not my thing syndrome	Operations settings lacking
	Operations culture of escalating decisions	Knowledge stock lacking	
	Operations rules lacking		
Attractiveness	*What service do we provide?*	*Do without anybody telling me*	*Who helps me grow?*
	Reactive, not proactive	Communication escalates little	Need stimulation to grow
	Waste of technical knowledge	Domino effect works badly	Lack of self-reflection
	Extended ecosystem	Feeling of very high occupancy	
	Sluggish contractor		
Engagement	*Operational targets*	*Values*	*Management style*
	Make them cross-reference	Honesty	
	Need more knowledge stock	Efficiency: get to the point	
		Closeness	

Designing the service jointly with the extended enterprise was an essential requirement. Hephaestus was not the client; for many measures it was just the extended enterprise. And any change in the service involved accepting joint work on both the design and use of technology. For example, changing the system for scheduling PIs meant working on capacities together with employees at the extended enterprise, and offering technological solutions to end customers.

The nine questions (Table 8.5) served to prove empirically that Hephaestus' operations culture was not in tune with what the CEO wanted to bring about. Alterations were needed to blend in with the proactiveness and service level the CEO requested. Causes for particular concern were the difficulties found in conveying to every Hephaestus participant the need to readjust and change in order to face up to future challenges. The CEO understood that the business environment would undergo alterations in a short space of time, and his aim was to take advantage of that to become the world's best company in the industry.

The nine questions revealed the need to delegate more responsibility and self-checking to middle management. For that reason, operations rules were defined, backed up by unlocking capacity through spotting primaries/secondaries and blending in with Constellation. Four service redesign projects have been started. Have they happened? Yes, somewhat. A way to go? Yes, they are getting there, since redesigning a service blended in with the extended enterprise cannot be done in a few months. It is hard step-by-step work, above all if technology must be incorporated and new client archetypes need to be adapted to. Hephaestus has an ingrained conceptual structure and has made things happen, as in the Emergency Unit or Cristina's Constellation. Others are going down their own implementation road.

Achilles

Achilles's work was distinct in that for a year they had been working on their Transformation Plan. They had spotted areas for improvement and designed measures to boost efficiency by inserting technology. They had a plan ready for the starting gun.

The support they sought in SPDM was a conceptual operations drive that included more intensive engagement throughout the company. G12 wanted it to be a plan; "of everybody, by everybody and for everybody". Indeed, they adopted that as a watchword and it became a much-used tag line.

As seen previously in other chapters, G12 became the epicenter and using knowledge as the main conceptual bulwark that SPDM introduced. The wish to transmit proactiveness by domino effect and get it across to all staff had spurred interesting communications measures and domino approaches. Let us look at some of them.

1. Appointing tutors. Every G12 member had six tutees under their wing, who in turn had 10–12 under theirs. This domino approach eased true transmission of every event under development.
2. Joint meetings of 70 tutees. The top tier of tutees met twice in plenary work sessions with G12. The aim was to transmit planning and the Transformation Plan's Gantt chart, take timely questions about its implementation and share concerns.[13] The CEO was present. G12 accepted the very personal challenge of showing the 70 their level of personal involvement, and how they relied on every one of them to implement the plan. Those two sessions were real benchmarks for the whole company, as in them an engaging and combative operations culture was drawn to meet the plan's targets.

---

[13] Some of the 70 needed a lot of help in order to absorb their role as pivots for the change.

3. Fortnightly meetings between the 70 tutees and their groups.
4. Meetings between the CEO and the whole staff. The CEO met to explain the Transformation Plan and then kick it off.
5. App showing plan's new developments. Anybody without a cellphone was given one so the entire staff could download an app to provide updates about the plan, detail progress with prototypes and keep all staff up to date.
6. Reports on the intranet about following up the plan.

G12 met weekly. Particularly important in its meetings was analyzing how communicating was done, what blockages existed and how to boost engagement. Progress with prototypes and everybody participating in their development came to underpin its success. I believe that this concern was one of the detonating factors in implementing the plan satisfactorily. Many of the 70 participated actively by making G12 presentations and became true champions of the plan. Their conviction stemmed from understanding how the different projects brought added value to both company and individual.

G12 was likewise a centerpiece. Although not all of its members were as keenly engaged, the tractive power of those who did stick up for their watchword has spawned a very positive attitude. Their standard-bearing and conviction about the way to go was crucial.

Several G12 members were also on the Board. Their desire to consolidate the operations culture that was budding within the Transformation Plan led them to ponder which of Achilles's weakness they might run into. They thus used the nine questions and their salient points are detailed in Table 8.6. In italics are the measures they prioritized and incorporated in the plan for solving.

Is There Anything New Under the Sun?

I have performed an exercise I find interesting. Drawing on Hephaestus' and Achilles's work, I have laid out the two Boards' answers in a table. Two wholly different companies, differently sized and from different sectors. Nonetheless, the answers show similarities.

Readers will not fail to notice that both companies' blockages are very similar to blockages in any company undergoing change. I must admit the issues often recur in every type of company in every type of sector.

Table 8.6 The Hephaestus Board of Directors' nine questions

	What must be done?	*Who have I assigned?*	*Who is in charge?*
Efficiency	Lack of prioritizing *Taking for granted what they must know how to do* *Absence of operations rules*	Conflict between tasks Lack of clear criteria for assignment Not making assignment explicit	Lack of clear responsibility Middle manager does not want underlings to stand out. No plural spirit
Attractiveness	*What service do we provide?*	*Do without anybody telling me*	*Who helps me grow?*
	Lack of cross-referenced service view Decisions not shared	Proactiveness lacking Feel work does not belong to them There are culprits There is no clear feedback	Not wanting to grow Not admitting to mistakes Not knowing who can help them to grow
Engagement	*Operational targets*	*Values*	*Management style*
	No real target measurement (passed down to underlings) Targets or how to measure them misunderstood	Dissenting behavior at times	Management style: fearless of mistakes, trusting, cooperative, educating Is next guy's knowledge respected?

A CEO told me the other day, "How tiresome it is to work with human beings" and, in truth, I agree very much. Perseverance and consistency are always my recommendations. And both teams have understood that.

They had to work without a break[14] to engage and engage. The only way, as we have been repeating, is to get each agent on board and have each one win something. This always goes hand in hand with an efficient operations structure and service design suited to the Promise. Personally, I am quite convinced that using the conceptual outline in the three SPDM levels is absolutely indispensable to make things happen (Table 8.7).

As a final indication in this chapter on engagement, I should like to share another tool I have seen used these past three years. Oddly, more in the case of Portuguese than Spanish companies.[15]

One of them, a big insurance company, has used blocking factors in the Promise and moments of truth (MTs) to channel and allow difficulties to surface that are inherent in changes the sector requires.[16] The moments of

---

[14] But without haste.

[15] Readers of my previous book will know that there is a Portuguese unit that uses the SPDM approach in its academic and consultancy work. "The nine questions" is one of their favorite tools.

[16] Insurance is another sector in the throes of great change. Clients are changing abruptly, new archetypes demand new solutions and accident rates are being modified. It is a sector that has made a lot of money and is very aware that in future the bonanza will not be what it was.

Table 8.7 Comparing answers from two Boards of Directors: Hephaestus and Achilles

	What must be done?		*Who have I assigned?*		*Who is in charge?*	
Efficiency	Everyday work grinds me down Domino effect to convey plans Operations culture of escalating decisions Operations rules lacking	Lack of prioritizing Taking for granted what they must know how to do Absence of operations rules	No feedback when responsibility not taken Not my thing syndrome Knowledge stock lacking	Conflict between tasks Lack of clear criteria for assignment Not making assignment explicit	Lack of operational decision-making Operations settings lacking	Lack of clear responsibility Middle manager does not want underlings to stand out. No plural spirit
	What service do we provide?		*Do without anybody telling me*		*Who helps me grow?*	
Attractiveness	Reactive, not proactive Waste of technical knowledge Extended ecosystem Sluggish contractor	Lack of cross-referenced service view Decisions not shared	Communication escalates little Domino effect works badly Feeling of very high occupancy	Proactiveness lacking Feel work does not belong to them There are culprits There is no clear feedback	Need stimulation to grow Lack of self-reflection	Not wanting to grow Not admitting to mistakes Not knowing who can help them to grow
	Operational targets		*Values*		*Management style*	
Engagement	Make them cross-reference Need more knowledge stock	No real target measurement (passed down to underlings) Targets or how to measure them misunderstood	Honesty Efficiency: get to the point Closeness	Dissenting behavior at times		Management style fearless of mistakes, trusting, cooperative, educating Is next guy's knowledge respected?

truth are moments where the service is at stake. Spotting them clarifies priorities and provides groups with criteria. By starting with the company's blockages so that the MTs can be positive, and by spotting blockages when fulfilling the Promise, the groups allowed a clear list to surface of joint measures to smash those blockages.

The way to use MTs follows the standard SPDM behavior that has already been explained. Choosing a representative management group, one-day jobs where methodology works as if framed to allow doubts to surface and every component to engage in seeking problems and solutions.

This focus was also used in the Portuguese company that wanted to servitize itself, and its success has helped the management board understand the great knowledge challenge they face.

SPDM Concepts Used in This Chapter

Chapter referred to: 14

The big idea in this chapter is the nine questions (Fig. 8.1). These questions are laid out in three rows. The first row tackles efficiency, the second the brain-power/company learning binomial and the third engaging brainpower in the organization.

What must be done?		What is assigned to me?		Who's in charge?
What service do we provide?		What must I do without being told?		Who will help me grow?
What goals do we have?		What values do we have?		What management style must we have?

Agreed work plan		Duties that everybody has assigned to them.		Levels of decision-making and responsibility.
The service's provisions and features.		Action criterion.		Learning development structure.
Operational goals.		Fixing and conveying company values.		Management style.

Fig. 8.1 SPDM nine questions outline

Figure 8.1 has two components of the nine questions. The first component is the questions per se. The second component describes the key issues each question must tackle.

Those questions are a wonderful guide to make any group think, and may be used in management groups or groups at other levels in an organization. They work flawlessly in any context. Using them at the start of a transformation job to spot existing blockages, as well as implementing the Promise's priorities, or to spot crucial aspects of a specific problem when fulfilling the service, all makes for a powerful engagement tool (point I in the Conceptual Appendix).

The chapter referred to above describes them in full detail. To avoid repetition, therefore, I shall skip that here.[17] In the appendix, I have included the tables suggested in the SPDM manual.

As the chapter's second topic, I include combining blockages in the nine questions with blockages that are specific to keeping the Promise (point II in the Conceptual Appendix). To perform such an analysis, it will suffice to list those elements that hinder applying the Promises's priorities to the service. Once said blockages are listed, we suggest classifying and ordering them by the impact they have on implementing the dimensions. Meaning, if a blockage primarily affects a dimension with a score of 4, it is more critical than if it affects an assessment with a score of 2. It is all a matter of prioritizing the action sequence, since whatever their valuation, blockages must go away.

The third issue focuses on doing the same exercise, but starting with the moments of truth. The aim is to spot what moments of truth affect fulfilling the Promise, which are most critical and, once again, spot the blockages they cause (point III in the Conceptual Appendix). These blockages are categorized according to the Promise's priorities.

All these tools have a great aim of totally engaging brainpower in action plans. And that can only be done if it is they that spot the blockages. Prioritizing the Promise in any of its three connotations enables focusing on priorities needed to fulfill the service strategy.

Chapter 8: Conceptual Appendix

I. The Nine Questions Structure

---

[17] And duplicating effort, and that flies in the face of efficiency. An unforgivable sin!

1. *What must be done?* Agreed work plan	2. *What is assigned to me?* Duties that everyone has assigned to them	3. *Who's in charge?* Levels of decision-making and responsibility
4. *What service do we provide?* The service's provisions and features	5. *What must I do without being told?* Action criterion	6. *Who will help me grow?* Learning development structure
7. *What goals do we have?* Operational goals	8. *What values do we have?* Fixing and conveying company values	9. *What management style must we have?* Management style

Derive the blocking factors from each questionnaire, put them together in numerical order and list them.

1	Agreed work plan
1	
1	
1	
2	Tasks assigned to each one
2	
2	
2	
3	Decision-making levels and responsibility
3	
3	
3	
4	Service provisions and features
4	
4	
4	
5	Criteria for action
5	
5	
5	
6	Structure for developing learning
6	
6	
6	
7	Operational targets
7	
7	
7	
8	Spot and transmit values
8	
8	
8	
9	Management style
9	
9	
9	

II. Problems Over Fulfilling the Promise

	COST Criterion Values	TIME Criterion Values	RANGE Criterion Values	INNOVATION Criterion Values	CONSISTENCY Criterion Values	VALUE TOTAL (Sum)
PROBLEMS						

- Add in the problems found in accomplishing the Mission (F.A6).
- Evaluate the blocking factors in line with the Mission's priorities. To do that:

  - Enter the Mission's dimensions/criteria/ratings at the top of F. B3.
  - Apply each criterion's rating to each blocking factor.
  - Add them up.

	Value	Value	Value	Value	Value	
Dimension	Cost	Time	Innovation	Range	Consistency	Total Scores
Criterion						
Problems with the promise						
P						0
P						0
P						0
P						0
P						0
P						0
P						0
P						0
Agreed work plan						
1						0
1						0
Tasks assigned to each one						
2						0
2						0
Decision-making levels and responsibility						
3						0
3						0
Service provisions and features						
4						0
4						0
Criteria for action						
5						0
5						0
Structure for developing learning						
6						0
6						0
Operational targets						
7						0
7						0
Spot and transmit company values						
8						0
8						0
Management style						
9						0
9						0

- Keep each blocking factor's original number (or P for the Mission's problems) but get rid of the questions and turn it into a running list.
- Now each blocking factor will have only its original number and rating.
- Rank them by score from the top-down.

P						0
P						0
P						0
P						0
1						0
1						0
2						0
2						0
3						0
3						0
4						0
4						0
5						0
5						0
6						0
6						0
7						0
7						0
8						0
8						0
9						0
9						0

- Use this list of top blocking factors to draw up action plans to eliminate them.

  - High- and low-rated blocking factors may come into play, but always stick to the spirit of high-rated ones.

- List the projects derived from the blocking factors and the nine questions.

III. Moments of Truth and Their Criticality When Fulfilling the Promise

Interaction points	MT
Moments when there is client interaction	Describe MTs

	COST	TIME	RANGE	INNOVATION	CONSISTENCY	TOTAL
	Criterion: Score	Criterion: Score	Criterion: Score	Criterion: Score	Criterion: Score	TOTAL SCORE (Sum)
MTs						

Problems that prevent finding MTs and become blockages.

		MT1 Score:	MT2 Score:	MT3 Score:	MT4 Score:	MT5 Score:
	Problems that are blockages					
1						
2						
3						
4						
5						
6						
7						
8						

9

Concluding Thoughts

Abstract To round off the SPDM journey for our four companies, this chapter provides concluding thoughts on key elements that may be summarized as a short guide to fixing service delivery problems.

The time has come to take a break, for some concluding thoughts.

Above all, I must say that SPDM is alive and well, is still being implemented and evolving. But I believe that the work done these past three years has made it even more totally applicable for getting results. Successfully adapting it to the world of these four companies, totally different in size as well as sector and structure,[1] has allowed a synthesis to be made.

A common denominator in the four companies: the need for engagement to achieve implementation. Nothing new under the sun. We have all been saying for years that you cannot get results unless your people are on board. He who does, knows. That is beyond question. Nothing gets done without the one who knows how.

But the temptation to act in fits and starts is very great. At times circumstances mean better financial results are needed right away and that may lead to drastic decisions. Tragic, too. That is part of our workaday world. No manager drops by my office without saying so. They need financial results right now; they have no time.

---

[1] And to many more through my students and managers at school. Every year, EMBA (IESE's Executive MBA program) students apply SPDM ideas to their companies because it is part of the course I teach. The results, so they tell me, are positive, although as there are grades involved I take that with a pinch of salt.

© The Author(s) 2019
B. Muñoz-Seca, *How to Get Things Right*, IESE Business Collection,
https://doi.org/10.1007/978-3-030-14088-5_9

The struggle to change this approach is titanic and entails a most serious problem. Getting things right, and sustainably, takes time and foresight. Elements that are not always handy. And very few have the vision required to act like our four companies. Pegasus had to tackle time compression, and introduced a group of 60 people to take that on. Artemis wanted to materialize the Family legacy and work with its top tier. Hephaestus wanted to act ahead of the troubles the market would bring its way, and engaged its management team and top tiers to design a new service proposition and enhance its efficiency. And Achilles needed to engage the whole organization to enact its Transformation Plan. Every CEO with a medium-term view, even though they might have situations that needed fixing urgently. Everybody saw that they needed method and commitment from their people to execute. Done by them, for them and for mutual gain.

Thinking of managers with short-term needs, my initial suggestions for thought will try to be very pragmatic.[2] If there is nothing else for it, combine a few unfortunate actions with value proposals. Moves that send a sustainable efficiency message. Draw up a mix that, in sum total, adds efficiency and learning for all. If not, your losses will be heavy.

Where there can be no compromise is in spotting the Promise, essence and flame red. An absolutely indispensable step, regardless of the situation a company is in.

This book presents several actions, within the SPDM framework, of great value and firm action. They require no great investment, and are instead methodological and focus on operations culture. But with very immediate effects. Let us see what they are.

- *Devise knowledge pills.* Use knowledge as the mainstay of efficiency and pills as a way to fill in gaps. Pills are a new way to transmit structured and applicative knowledge to perform concrete tasks. Based on individual pride in performing tasks better than the rest, they are easy to make and cheap. And most effective, according to the ongoing study at Achilles. Efficiency, cost-cutting and steepening the learning curve. It does not get any better than that!
- *Analyzing individual consumption and spotting primaries and secondaries.* If you cannot send the "No fire, No fire" message, at least help to get across the capacity analysis method. The phrase "I have no time"[3] must be absolutely and totally wiped out. Performing a methodological capacity analysis is within everybody's grasp. Brainpower is interested in knowing where they consume time. Unlocking capacity, or at least understanding what time is wasted on, adds value. The message must be built up positively, and linked to pills. Knowing who consumes least, so they may teach and be a benchmark.

---

[2] Then I shall think for those who do have time for foresight.
[3] And meanwhile, wipe out NO.

- *Industrialize as much as possible.* Brainpower gets irritated over inefficiency. That irritation must be harnessed to brush off all the filth, and clean up. It is a message everybody understands. And do that with your people, not outsiders. Achilles's methodological drivers or Pegasus's "special forces" are examples to follow. They absorbed SPDM, made it their own and incorporated it into their everyday tasks. There is always brainpower ready to push; at Artemis they cropped up in unsuspected places and at Hephaestus the will to modify the service value proposal got many to work together. The aim is efficiency and value added; the way is methodological questioning.
- *Spotting interruptions and smashing them.* They are easily found and their "marketing" effect on constructive efficiency is most important.
- *Establish plans and rolling forecasts* with the CEO's hallmark. It is absolutely essential to know what incoming demand will be, spot today's problems and tomorrow's, and make certain forecasts. Achilles and Pegasus are good examples of this measure's impact. The CEO has been actively involved in both as a fundamental element of commitment.

Now let us delve into more leisurely thoughts for those who can look ahead with some peace of mind. Above all, as we have seen in this book, be very clear on what every player gets out of it. In terms of knowledge, freedom, whatever. But explain it. That becomes a driver for innosufferers and gets them to accept doing things in another way.

Then, understanding that the SPDM model brings order to the tangle of efficiency and cost-cutting messages that any manager faces. There are many issues to tackle and their effect on each other, unsuspected. Figure 9.1 shows some of the operational strategy challenges faced by a company's management. SPDM provides a methodological structure and new ideas to tackle them.

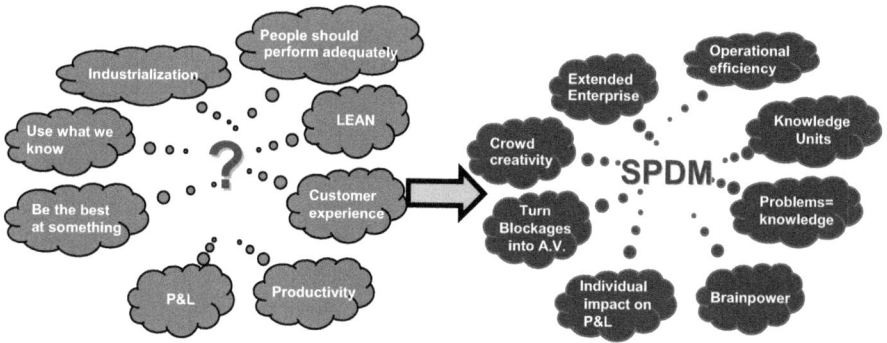

Fig. 9.1 Operational efficiency and sustainability using SPDM

This book details SPDM ideas that have been used by our four companies. Among them, I should like to stress those I deem most relevant for individual consideration.

- One of my mantras, which I cannot avoid. Establish self-checking as TREASURE did at Achilles. That spawns learning and improvement.
- Specify the service, while understanding the knowledge portfolio needed to deliver it. Banish the "lack of quality" concept and turn it into fulfilling comprehensible and measurable specifications. The clearer it is, the more KISS it is. And the easier to implant and follow up. CEC has shown that.
- *Spotting popups to make prototypes.* Solutions spawned for deep-seated problems. They are a wonderful way to show how creativity can bring differential and redirect it. Prototyping is another big lesson learned these past three years. Prototyping convinces the whole organization.
- *Establish methodological drivers the Achilles way.* They are convinced that knowledge is the mainstay of efficiency. Using them, lean actions may be consolidated, efficiency improved and every agent gets to grow. Their "think different" (or think outside the box) approach is crucial to turning blocking factors into value added. They may be the champions of design service.
- *Set up a tracks and modules pilot* scheme in a department where tracks and modules may be easily established. BOs are perfect. They usually come with very structured problems that enable understanding and make results stand out right away. If you have no BO, use an area where a high percentage of problems are structured and where this suggested functioning may be introduced. Brainpower thrives on tracks. They get it and tracks challenge them. Modules may be somewhat difficult at first, but send a message to eliminate waste and of indispensable clarity to achieve the streamlining that leads to sustainability.
- Spot Himalayas and work with them to engage them. They are high value-added brainpower that needs to be steered back into the organization.
- Implant a mini Constellation to show the way to go is developing value-added tasks, and "No hire, No fire". As at Hephaestus, a prototype in a highly visible area serves as an internal benchmark. Facts are facts, talk is cheap.
- Set up a couple of Knowledge Unit prototypes Pegasus-style, while incorporating the extended enterprise, if possible. They are focal points for spawning new ideas, spotting clients' latent demands and proposing new services.

- Use the nine questions, like Hephaestus, Artemis, Achilles and Pegasus, to spot blockages and proposals for improvement. That comes with understanding implementation distance in order to spot knowledge gaps.

I cannot finish without mentioning the project chief's particular role. Choosing somebody who shares SPDM operational culture is absolutely critical. Clarity, simplicity, pragmatism and focus must be some of their attributes. I shall highlight three out of the four project chiefs. The CEO decided the fourth had to be changed half-way through the project. And that is always very negative. The substitute could not pick up the project's pace. Other members of the group were better pacemakers.

Just like every participant, project chiefs must spot what everybody gains on a personal level. The Achilles, Hephaestus and Pegasus project chiefs had totally different personalities, but similar archetype traits. All-rounders, drivers, patient, who know how to listen and fall on their feet, and sense everything that everybody needs telling at the right time.[4] And that persevere. That must be a widespread trait in any SPDM project. Constancy and follow-up. Remember: "Talk is cheap, facts come to stay." And showing realities is indispensable. "A thousand $1,000-improvements" has always been a basic part of the SPDM approach. And that entails extracting realities from any opportunity to improve.

In SPDM they saw a way to derive solutions from problems they knew were deep seated. And get tangible results. What did they get out of it on a personal level? Well, above all, I believe the pleasure of a job well done and meeting a challenge. They are great professionals and want to see progress. Obviously, recognition by the AD and possibly hidden agendas I am not aware of.[5] Always, win-win. Individuals and company. Always.

I end the book here. As a parting thought, I suggest using SPDM to glimpse and understand what is still on the to-do list (this chapter's conceptual index includes the SPDM Manual's final form). And some personal recommendations,[6] between you, dear reader, and I.

Remember sustainability in Operations is gaged by the contribution margin. Spotting deviations and alterations in it serves as a great indicator of the operational structure's health, robustness and worth.

---

[4] Does it show that I have a weakness for them? Well I do. They are three wonderful people, whom I have grown personally fond of. It usually happens with people I think the world of; it is a real pleasure to work with them.

[5] But totally positive, as they have made the projects succeed.

[6] Excuse me if I make so bold. I make recommendations all day and cannot end this book without making some. Furthermore, if you have read my last two books, I feel close and would like to offer you, if I may, some personal recommendations.

If you can, set up a P&L for each person in your organization so that they know what their work contributes, and understand the value added which that involves. Stress the need for a common vocabulary and set up operations rules, so your people do not work by common sense. Use brainpower to contribute value added and, if the business case allows, hand over F5 tasks to technology. Finally, work on engaging everybody.

The examples given in this book may help to guide you. That has been my aim. Demonstrate using facts and actions. Using real-life examples. And do not forget to set up an operations culture of trust and transparency, as they are the basis for sustainable productivity and efficiency.

I bid farewell by wishing you all the wonderful operating dreams that come true! I hope to have contributed ideas to make that happen.

Chapter 9: Conceptual Appendix

SPDM checklist		
	Agree ✓	Pending x
1. Define promise, essence, flame red and MTs		
Define the promise		
Translating the Promise's five dimensions into criteria and prioritizing them		
Define essence		
Define flame red		
Spot MTs and specify critical ones		
2. Proactiveness		
Nine questions		
Twenty commandments		
3. Spot knowledge I need today and tomorrow		

Spot what I know today
    Settings for problems equals knowledge
    Do I have a KDB?
    What I must know and what the extended enterprise must know
    KU		

Spot what I must know today (knowledge gaps)
    Have I translated problems I have into knowledge needs?
    Have I found the knowledge level I need using VOC indexing?		

Spot what I need to know tomorrow
    Impact of new problems and services
    Have I spotted projects I want to face in the company in the innovation matrix?
    Have I spotted the agent profiles according to their role within the innovation?
    Have I thought how I must acquire the knowledge I do not have and need to bring excellence to the service?		

4. Operations		
Define tasks by processor and occupancy rates		
Distinguish between primary and secondary tasks		
Spot the company's critical processes		
Industrializing as much as possible without losing essence		
Spot the agent profile needed to provide the service		

Spot blocking factors that prevent me giving the service as promised
    Is a formal problem-solving system defined?
    Is an informal problem-solving system defined?
    Are formal and informal information systems defined?		

5. Service design		
Redesign the concept to smash blocks in competitiveness		
Analysis of conflicting points in settings		
Spot latent demand		
6. Enabling improvement		
Spot root causes of problems		
Criticality of problems		
Support creativity		
Innovation roles		
Learning from service improvements		
Design the training plan system		
7. Implement SPDM express		
Choose visible unit and make it a benchmark		
Prototyping implementation by following milestones		
Share results with organization using quick wins		

Glossary

A

Agile Model Operations model that focuses on marketing products quickly by using modular production and cooperation between companies. It focuses, moreover, on eliminating avoidable uncertainty, having a plan B for residual uncertainty, striving for zero-minute delivery time and an operational structure with room for maneuver.

Area 20 Group of wise men and women picked for the Achilles CSM project.

Attractiveness Degree to which people are satisfied in the organization, basically due to what they get out of it. Focuses on watching over an individual's learning process. Smooths out the learning process and steers it toward a win-win situation for the individual and the organization.

Autoritas Moral authority somebody earns by their own merits and knowledge.

B

Blocking factors Factors that prevent achieving goals that have been set.

Bottleneck Processor that produces least, one that thus limits the number of clients or actions that all the other processors can undertake in the same period of time, and holds up the service.

Brainpower As opposed to manpower. In the twenty-first century brains are employed that need different management styles to manpower.

C

Capacity Hours a processor is available.

CSM (Client Specifications Materialization) Achilles project to define specifications for contracted services.

© The Author(s) 2019
B. Muñoz-Seca, *How to Get Things Right*, IESE Business Collection,
https://doi.org/10.1007/978-3-030-14088-5

Customer journey Tool used to visualize how a client experiences the service by interacting with the people and structures that deliver it. It breaks down the service into five phases (know, involve, use, extend and quit) and cross-references it with the touchpoints the client is exposed to.

D

DNP SAS activity aimed at spotting clients' hidden and latent demand.

E

Efficiency Extent to which an organization solves operational problems properly and reaches desired goals. Focuses on action to solve today's problems and those that lead to improving productivity in Operations.

Employability Individual knowledge stock that adds value in order to find employment.

Essence A company's DNA.

Everest Achilles Knowledge Unit focused on solving exploratory problems with implementing Everest software.

Exploration Mechanism for producing ideas that consist of gradual changes in conceptual structure, by systematically applying transformations that are known but used unusually.

Extended enterprise Joining together suppliers, distributors, companies and clients to shape the service as an interrelated whole (Kanter, 1999).

F

F&B (Food&Beverage) Catering sector term used to denote all activities comprising the restaurant industry.

Facts Achilles Knowledge Unit focused on solving problems with harmonizing data.

Five-Star Constellation Action that links each agent's occupancy rate to their knowledge stock and knowledge gaps, to execute today's and tomorrow's service tasks (problems).

Flame Red Fundamental that makes the essence operational. The element that sets our company apart from the rest, making it unique and giving it its own identity.

FTE (Full Time Equivalent) Way to calculate numbers of people assigned to workstations when they work less than eight hours per day.

G

Golden Triad Three complementary and synergetic mainstays for action (efficiency, attractiveness and engagement) that make up the SPDM operating culture.

H

Himalaya (syndrome) Brainpower doing its own thing and acting as it sees fit, convinced that it is doing its best to reach the target set, or for the company.

I

I-CAN Achilles project that analyzes knowledge and adapts it to tasks. It ends up with a plan to unlock capacity by improving efficiency.

Individual (P&L) earnings statement Tool reflecting the repercussions of individual actions on the company's overall P&L.

Industry 4.0 Implementation of the fourth industrial revolution, which is making human resources disappear to create a wholly technological environment.

Innomanager One of three agents involved in innovation; the one in charge of making innovation succeed.

Innosufferer One of three agents involved in innovation; the one who ends up suffering and/or noticing the effects of innovation on their job. Leading player in implementation for getting it right.

Interruption An agent halting an ongoing task to perform another. Interruptions kill productivity, the creative process or the capacity to learn.

K

KDB (Knowledge Data Base) Database where knowledge is stored.

KISS (keep it simple and stupid) Approach aimed at performing jobs and activities in the simplest possible way.

KJ Method Bottom-up approach devised by Shoji Shiba, which starts off by listing concepts that have pictures in common.

Knowledge "Circumstance or condition to apprehend the truth or facts by means of reason", in the SPDM model we dub it a problem.

Knowledge Gap Difference between the knowledge base an agent has and the knowledge needed to solve a given problem (Muñoz-Seca and Riverola, 2003).

Knowledge Hub Hub from where knowledge is provided to different actors.

Knowledge Pill Knowledge to be transferred to specific jobs for solving specific problems. The way to transfer it is by using YouTube videos no more than three minutes long.

Knowledge Stock Stock of knowledge that a company has materialized and is stored in its agents' brains.

KPI (*Key Performance Indicator*) Indicator to measure progress adapted to activity according to design.

KU (Knowledge Unit) Knowledge clusters comprising different individuals from different parts of the organization whose common link is the similarity of knowledge types that they pool in job skills. They focus on solving novel exploratory problems in the company.

L

Layout Physical arrangement of the place where a service is provided.

Lean Model Operations model focused on eliminating waste by assessing all types of it, spending on nothing that is not needed, standardizing, keeping operations on the same track, balancing the load and making results public.

LTA (Long-Term Average) Way to calculate job consumption in service companies.

M

Matrix, Capacity Method for finding client output.

Matrix, Load Given x production, it allows each processor's utilization rate to be found.

MIX Percentage breakdown of service demand. It must add up to 100%.

Muda Wastefulness in Japanese.

N

NDA (Non-Disclosure Agreement) Agreement reached by Achilles G12 to restrict use of G12 discussions.

Nine questions Tool to find blocking factors in the organization that hinder implementing SPDM operational culture and fulfilling the Promise.

O

Observation First step in the scientific method. It consists of closely observing a phenomenon, fact or event, and recording information to study afterward.

Operations All activities that range from an idea to a satisfied client.

Operations rules Encapsulated happenings providing guidelines and specifying priorities for making the system coherent.

Out of the Box, thinking Thinking outside the usual mechanisms to find differential models for action.

P

Persona Ethnographic model that describes the client's anthropological features.

PI Periodic inspection by Hephaestus to determine clients' gas consumption. The activity is undertaken by subcontractors in the extended enterprise ecosystem.

Popup Innovation that emerges spontaneously to resolve a conflictive situation.

Potestas Authority an organizational structure confers on each position.

Problem Situation somebody finds unpleasant.

Processor Agent that does the job.

Promise Translating strategy into concrete elements to enable Operations settings.

Prototype Turning ideas into real services that are tested, repeated and perfected.

Q

Quality Complying with the service specification; complying with the service's technical features.

R

Rho (ρ) Greek letter used to denote each processor's utilization rate.

Rolling forecast Periodic review of forecast demand to adjust forecasts in line with events.

S

Service Activities Sequence (SAS) Model for setting up a services structure comprising seven activities split up into three groups: service design, operational infrastructure and providing and maintaining the service. It describes activities involved in transforming an ever-changing idea of service provision.

Service dream Way that senior management envisions how the service should be provided, what worthwhile components should be delivered and how they must stand out. It focuses on the action of providing service to clients.

Service module Cluster of activities that have a joint identity and make up a core.

Service MTs (Moments of Truth) Differential service moments that, when spotted, add value to assess client satisfaction with the service displayed. They are the services critical points.

Servitization All companies are service companies and the purely industrial ones must spot their service components to add them to their value proposal.

SIC (Service Innovation Cycle) A SAS cycle that links the Demand for New Provisions (DNP) to spawning new services.

SLA (Service Level Agreement) Service indicators used to measure suppliers' actions and specified in contracts.

SPDM (Service Problem-Driven Management) Model aimed at overall Operations settings, the mainstay for conceptual development in the services area, designed by Muñoz-Seca in 2016.

Strategic implementation The most abstract level in the SPDM model, consisting of three elements: Promise, essence and flame red.

T

Task, Primary Task requiring a zero-minute response time.

Task, Secondary Task that may be performed whenever it suits a processor or the latter has a lull between serving clients.

Touchpoint (TP) Along the customer journey, determining the journey's critical interaction moments.

TPS (Toyota Production System) Japanese production system implemented by Toyota Motor Corp. focused on, among other things, using only what is needed when it is needed, and constant problem-solving.

Track Problems freeway, quick and perfectly delineated track along which certain types of problems may drive.

TREASURE Achilles project to materialize/broadcast knowledge and make it available to the organization. It also entails learning by mistakes.

Tribe Bundling of archetypes that make up an ethnographic client unit.

Twenty Commandments 20 rules that comprise SPDM operations culture.

V

VOC (Verb-Object-Condition) Structure for indexing knowledge that allows it to be retrieved based on any of these three components.

W

Win-Win Indispensable premise for implementing SPDM. The company wins and the individual wins.

Bibliography

Boden, M. A. (1991). *The creative mind: Myths and mechanisms* (1st ed.). New York: Basic Books. (First edition published 1990 by George Weidenfeld and Nicolson Ltd.)

Brown, T., & Wyatt, J. (2010). Design thinking for social innovation. *Standford Innovation Review, Winter, 8*(1).

Machado, J. (2018). *Parques de Sintra-Montes da Lua*. P-A-1495 AESE Business School-Portugal.

Muñoz-Seca, B. (2008). *An approach to facilitate problem solving: Individualizing the problem proposition*. Research paper no 768. IESE.

Muñoz-Seca, B. (2017). *How to make things happen*. Cham: Palgrave Macmillan.

Muñoz-Seca, B., & Silva Santiago, C. (2003). *Four dimensions to induce learning: The challenge profile*. Research paper no 520. IESE.

Moss Kanter, R. (1999). Change is everyone's job: Managing the extended enterprise in a globally connected world. *Organizational Dynamics, 28*(1), 7–23.

NASA. (2017). https://nasasearch.nasa.gov/search/images?affiliate=nasa&query=constellation

Ries, E. (2011). *The lean startup: How today's entrepreneurs use continuous innovation to create radically successful businesses*. New York: Crown Business, Random House.

© The Author(s) 2019

B. Muñoz-Seca, *How to Get Things Right*, IESE Business Collection,

https://doi.org/10.1007/978-3-030-14088-5

Index[1]

---

[1] Note: Page numbers followed by 'n' refer to notes.

© The Author(s) 2019
B. Muñoz-Seca, *How to Get Things Right*, IESE Business Collection,
https://doi.org/10.1007/978-3-030-14088-5